THIS BOOK BELONGS TO

START DATE

SHE READS TRUTH

SHE READS TRUTH™

ISBN 978-1-952670-94-7

1 2 3 4 5 6 7 8 9 10

Verses omitted in the CSB are also omitted in this book.

Research support provided by Logos Bible Software™. Learn more at logos.com.

This book was printed offset in Nashville, Tennessee, on 70# Lynx Opaque. Cover is 100# Cougar Opaque with a soft touch lamination.

MATTHEW

The story that unfolds in
Matthew isn't just for us to read.
We're meant to respond!

Tameshia Williams, ThM
CONTENT MARKETING STRATEGIST

I love getting lost in a great book. I'll plop into my favorite chair, a gray-green rocker recliner, worn in from years of reading. (I'm pretty sure it's holding all of my missing socks hostage.) Hours feel like mere minutes as I transition through various sitting postures, eagerly turning the page in anticipation of plot twists and turns. And as with any good story, the ending comes far too soon.

What about you? Are you also captivated by the power of story? I hope your answer is yes! Because we're about to spend four weeks immersed in the greatest story of all time.

In the book of Matthew, we're introduced to Jesus not from a historian or reporter, but through the eyes of one of his earliest disciples. Matthew takes us into the world of the first century as God's people waited for the promised Messiah. The Gospel's earliest scenes reveal God's faithfulness to keep that promise. Jesus is born, and everything changes.

Maybe you've read the book of Matthew before, or maybe it's your first time. But don't you love how God's Word holds something new for the repeat reader and newcomer alike? Matthew's Gospel is an invitation for us to get to know Jesus over and over again through key moments from His life and ministry on earth. He preached good news, declaring that the "kingdom of heaven has come near" (Mt 4:17). He taught and modeled what life in the kingdom of God looks like. He healed the sick and engaged the marginalized with compassion. He performed miracles among multitudes. He challenged religious rulers and displayed authority over forces of darkness.

The story that unfolds in Matthew isn't just for us to read. We're meant to respond! The Savior of the world gave His life, dying on the cross for our sins and offering life to all those who repent and turn to Him. (See more in "Faith and Belief" on page 16.)

What are your greatest needs today, your greatest longings? Whatever they are, I pray that each day's reading will continually remind you that Jesus is the only one who can fulfill them. So grab your favorite reading spot and settle in, friend. A grand story is waiting for you.

ON PURPOSE

DESIGN *on* PURPOSE

At She Reads Truth, we believe in pairing the inherently beautiful Word of God with the aesthetic beauty it deserves. Each of our resources is thoughtfully and artfully designed to highlight the beauty, goodness, and truth of Scripture in a way that reflects the themes of each curated reading plan.

DESIGN

The photographs in this book call us to experience this familiar Gospel with a fresh wind. The centerpiece of the imagery is fabric blowing in the wind, a concept inspired by the ways the truth of the gospel affects every aspect of our lives. As the fabric flows in whatever direction the wind takes it, so do our lives follow and surrender to the ways of God's kingdom as demonstrated by Jesus's teachings and His life.

The botanical, floral, and nature images throughout the book represent Jesus's life on earth, while the images of sky and clouds allude to His resurrection. The color palette is fresh and lively, reminiscent of the joy and hope found in the resurrection.

HOW TO USE THIS BOOK

She Reads Truth is a community of women dedicated to reading the Word of God every day. In this **Matthew** reading plan, we will read the Gospel of Matthew, along with complementary passages of Scripture, as we get to know the life, ministry, death, and resurrection of Jesus Christ, the Savior of the world.

READ & REFLECT

Your **Matthew** book focuses primarily on Scripture, with added features to come alongside your time with God's Word.

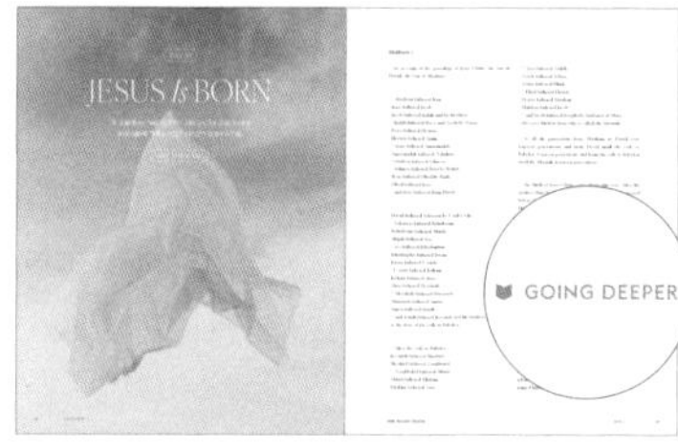

SCRIPTURE READING

Designed for a Monday start, this book presents the book of Matthew in daily readings, along with additional passages curated to show how the theme of the main reading can be found throughout Scripture.

Additional passages are marked in your daily reading with the Going Deeper heading.

REFLECTION QUESTIONS

This reading plan features questions and space for personal reflection.

COMMUNITY & CONVERSATION

You can start reading this book at any time! If you want to join women from Lincoln to Latvia as they read along with you, the She Reads Truth community will start Day 1 of **Matthew** on Monday, March 4, 2024.

SHE READS TRUTH APP

Devotionals corresponding to each daily reading can be found in the **Matthew** reading plan on the She Reads Truth app. New devotionals will be published each weekday once the plan begins on Monday, March 4, 2024. You can use the app to participate in community discussion and more.

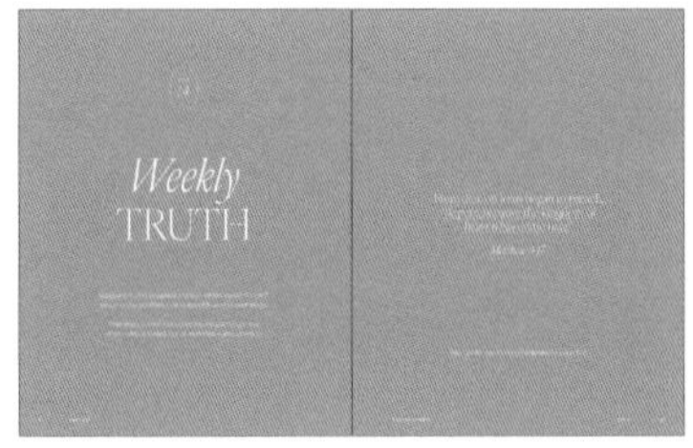

GRACE DAY

Use the first three Saturdays to catch up on your reading, pray, and rest in the presence of the Lord.

The final days of this Matthew reading plan walk through the events of the crucifixion and resurrection. No matter where you are in the calendar year, we invite you to reflect and remember this holy weekend as you read.

WEEKLY TRUTH

The first three Sundays are set aside for Scripture memorization.

See tips for memorizing Scripture on page 132.

EXTRAS

This book features additional tools to help you gain a deeper understanding of the text.

Find a complete list of extras on pages 10–11.

SHEREADSTRUTH.COM

The **Matthew** reading plan and devotionals will also be available at SheReadsTruth.com as the community reads each day. Invite your family, friends, and neighbors to read along with you!

SHE READS TRUTH PODCAST

Subscribe to the She Reads Truth podcast and join our founders and their guests each week as they talk about what you'll read in the week ahead.

*Podcast episodes 215–218 for our **Matthew** series release on Mondays beginning March 4, 2024.*

TABLE *of*

CONTENTS

WEEK 03

WEEK 04

Key Verse

FROM *then on*
Jesus BEGAN
to PREACH,
"REPENT, *because*
the KINGDOM
of HEAVEN *has*
come NEAR."

MATTHEW 4:17

She Reads MATTHEW

Time to Read Matthew

2 HOURS 21 MINUTES

On the Timeline

Matthew was written in the first century, around AD 60, before the fall of the temple in Jerusalem in AD 70. The events recorded in Matthew took place during the life of Christ, between roughly 5 BC and AD 33.

A Little Background

Though no author is identified in the text, the early Church unanimously affirmed that the apostle Matthew authored the Gospel of Matthew. Most scholars believe that Matthew used Mark's Gospel when writing his own. If this is correct, Matthew's Gospel was written after Mark's, though the date of Mark's Gospel is also a bit of a mystery. Irenaeus (ca AD 180) claimed that Mark wrote his Gospel after Peter's death in the mid-AD 60s. However, Clement of Alexandria, who wrote only twenty years after Irenaeus, claimed that Mark wrote his Gospel while Peter was still alive.

Message & Purpose

It seems fitting that the first book of the New Testament begins with the words: "An account of the genealogy of Jesus Christ." This Gospel was written from a strong Jewish perspective to show that Jesus truly is the Messiah and coming King promised in the Old Testament.

Matthew presents an eyewitness testimony of the ministry of Jesus and emphasizes certain theological truths:

01 Jesus is the Messiah, the long-awaited King of God's people.

02 Jesus is the new Abraham, the founder of a new spiritual Israel consisting of all people (both Jews and Gentiles) who follow Him.

03 Jesus is the new Moses, the deliverer, instructor, and mediator of God's people.

04 Jesus is Immanuel, the virgin-born Son of God who fulfills the promises of the Old Testament.

Give Thanks for the Gospel of Matthew

As the first book in the NT, the Gospel of Matthew serves as a gateway between the Old and New Testaments. Of the NT books, and certainly of the four Gospels, Matthew makes the most direct connections to the OT. Matthew looks forward by discussing not only the Messiah's coming and His ministry, but also His future plan for His Church and kingdom.

FAITH *and* BELIEF

Faith and belief are key themes throughout the Gospel of Matthew, and these themes are intrinsically linked to one another. Jesus observes when they are present and when they are lacking. He calls His disciples to operate out of faith. But perhaps words like *faith* and *belief* have become so familiar, we forget the weight of what it really means to live by faith—to believe and let our actions flow from that belief.

The Greek noun *pistis*, translated as "faith," means conviction of the truth. For the Christ follower, faith is confidence and utmost trust in Jesus Himself. The Greek word *pisteuo*, translated as "belief," is the verb form of pistis. It describes the action of faith, moving beyond a mental acknowledgment of God to the action of believing. Belief means that we actively place our trust in Jesus.

As we journey through the book of Matthew we will take a closer look at moments of faith and belief along the way. How does Jesus talk about faith? What did it look like for people to act in faith? How are we prompted to respond in belief?

We'll see Jesus remind us that our goal isn't just having more faith. After all, only a mustard seed's (that's small!) worth of faith in Him can move mountains (Mt 17:20). So it comes down not to the amount of faith we can muster, but a focus on who we are putting our faith in.

Faith is evidenced when we lean into what we know to be true, when we walk in the confidence of trusting Christ—even if it's only a mustard seed's worth.

Keep an eye out for the mustard seed icons as you go. These are places to stop and reflect on where we see faith at work in the text. These aren't all the examples from Matthew, but a few key places to note and make observations. At each of these stops you'll find prompts to guide your reflection along with space to jot down notes.

You'll have two opportunities for extended reflection on faith and belief: one at the end of Week 2 and one on Resurrection Sunday as we conclude the book of Matthew.

DAY 01

JESUS *Is* BORN

You are to name him Jesus, because he will save his people from their sins.

MATTHEW 1:21

Matthew 1

THE GENEALOGY OF JESUS CHRIST

[1] An account of the genealogy of Jesus Christ, the Son of David, the Son of Abraham:

FROM ABRAHAM TO DAVID

[2] Abraham fathered Isaac,
Isaac fathered Jacob,
Jacob fathered Judah and his brothers,
[3] Judah fathered Perez and Zerah by Tamar,
Perez fathered Hezron,
Hezron fathered Aram,
[4] Aram fathered Amminadab,
Amminadab fathered Nahshon,
Nahshon fathered Salmon,
[5] Salmon fathered Boaz by Rahab,
Boaz fathered Obed by Ruth,
Obed fathered Jesse,
[6] and Jesse fathered King David.

FROM DAVID TO THE BABYLONIAN EXILE

David fathered Solomon by Uriah's wife,
[7] Solomon fathered Rehoboam,
Rehoboam fathered Abijah,
Abijah fathered Asa,
[8] Asa fathered Jehoshaphat,
Jehoshaphat fathered Joram,
Joram fathered Uzziah,
[9] Uzziah fathered Jotham,
Jotham fathered Ahaz,
Ahaz fathered Hezekiah,
[10] Hezekiah fathered Manasseh,
Manasseh fathered Amon,
Amon fathered Josiah,
[11] and Josiah fathered Jeconiah and his brothers
at the time of the exile to Babylon.

FROM THE EXILE TO THE MESSIAH

[12] After the exile to Babylon
Jeconiah fathered Shealtiel,
Shealtiel fathered Zerubbabel,
[13] Zerubbabel fathered Abiud,
Abiud fathered Eliakim,
Eliakim fathered Azor,
[14] Azor fathered Zadok,
Zadok fathered Achim,
Achim fathered Eliud,
[15] Eliud fathered Eleazar,
Eleazar fathered Matthan,
Matthan fathered Jacob,
[16] and Jacob fathered Joseph the husband of Mary,
who gave birth to Jesus who is called the Messiah.

[17] So all the generations from Abraham to David were
fourteen generations; and from David until the exile to
Babylon, fourteen generations; and from the exile to Babylon
until the Messiah, fourteen generations.

THE NATIVITY OF THE MESSIAH

[18] The birth of Jesus Christ came about this way: After his
mother Mary had been engaged to Joseph, it was discovered
before they came together that she was pregnant from the
Holy Spirit. [19] So her husband, Joseph, being a righteous
man, and not wanting to disgrace her publicly, decided to
divorce her secretly.

[20] But after he had considered these things, an angel of the
Lord appeared to him in a dream, saying, "Joseph, son of
David, don't be afraid to take Mary as your wife, because
what has been conceived in her is from the Holy Spirit.
[21] She will give birth to a son, and you are to name him Jesus,
because he will save his people from their sins."

[22] Now all this took place to fulfill what was spoken by the
Lord through the prophet:

> [23] See, the virgin will become pregnant
> and give birth to a son,
> and they will name him Immanuel,

which is translated "God is with us."

[24] When Joseph woke up, he did as the Lord's angel had
commanded him. He married her [25] but did not have sexual
relations with her until she gave birth to a son. And he
named him Jesus.

Matthew 2

WISE MEN VISIT THE KING

1 After Jesus was born in Bethlehem of Judea in the days of King Herod, wise men from the east arrived in Jerusalem, 2 saying, "Where is he who has been born king of the Jews? For we saw his star at its rising and have come to worship him."

3 When King Herod heard this, he was deeply disturbed, and all Jerusalem with him. 4 So he assembled all the chief priests and scribes of the people and asked them where the Messiah would be born.

5 "In Bethlehem of Judea," they told him, "because this is what was written by the prophet:

> 6 And you, Bethlehem, in the land of Judah,
> are by no means least among the rulers of Judah:
> Because out of you will come a ruler
> who will shepherd my people Israel."

7 Then Herod secretly summoned the wise men and asked them the exact time the star appeared. 8 He sent them to Bethlehem and said, "Go and search carefully for the child. When you find him, report back to me so that I too can go and worship him."

9 After hearing the king, they went on their way. And there it was—the star they had seen at its rising. It led them until it came and stopped above the place where the child was. 10 When they saw the star, they were overwhelmed with joy. 11 Entering the house,

they saw the child with Mary his mother, and falling to their knees, they worshiped him.

Then they opened their treasures and presented him with gifts: gold, frankincense, and myrrh. 12 And being warned in a dream not to go back to Herod, they returned to their own country by another route.

THE FLIGHT INTO EGYPT

13 After they were gone, an angel of the Lord appeared to Joseph in a dream, saying, "Get up! Take the child and his mother, flee to Egypt, and stay there until I tell you. For Herod is about to search for the child to kill him." 14 So he got up, took the child and his mother during the night, and escaped to Egypt. 15 He stayed there until Herod's death, so that what was spoken by the Lord through the prophet might be fulfilled: Out of Egypt I called my Son.

THE MASSACRE OF THE INNOCENTS

16 Then Herod, when he realized that he had been outwitted by the wise men, flew into a rage. He gave orders to massacre all the boys in and around Bethlehem who were two years old and under, in keeping with the time he had learned from the wise men. 17 Then what was spoken through Jeremiah the prophet was fulfilled:

18 A voice was heard in Ramah,

> weeping, and great mourning,
> Rachel weeping for her children;
> and she refused to be consoled,
> because they are no more.

THE RETURN TO NAZARETH

19 After Herod died, an angel of the Lord appeared in a dream to Joseph in Egypt, 20 saying, "Get up, take the child and his mother, and go to the land of Israel, because those who intended to kill the child are dead." 21 So he got up, took the child and his mother, and entered the land of Israel. 22 But when he heard that Archelaus was ruling over Judea in place of his father Herod, he was afraid to go there. And being warned in a dream, he withdrew to the region of Galilee. 23 Then he went and settled in a town called Nazareth to fulfill what was spoken through the prophets, that he would be called a Nazarene.

GOING DEEPER

NOTES

Micah 5:1–4

FROM DEFEATED RULER TO CONQUERING KING

1 Now, daughter who is under attack,
you slash yourself in grief;
a siege is set against us!
They are striking the judge of Israel
on the cheek with a rod.
2 Bethlehem Ephrathah,
you are small among the clans of Judah;
one will come from you
to be ruler over Israel for me.
His origin is from antiquity,
from ancient times.
3 Therefore, Israel will be abandoned until the time
when she who is in labor has given birth;
then the rest of the ruler's brothers will return
to the people of Israel.
4 He will stand and shepherd them
in the strength of the LORD,
in the majestic name of the LORD his God.
They will live securely,
for then his greatness will extend
to the ends of the earth.

John 1:14

The Word became flesh and dwelt among us. We observed his glory, the glory as the one and only Son from the Father, full of grace and truth.

JESUS (DAY 02) *Prepares for* MINISTRY

Matthew 3

THE HERALD OF THE MESSIAH

1 In those days John the Baptist came, preaching in the wilderness of
Judea 2 and saying, "Repent, because the kingdom of heaven has come
near!" 3 For he is the one spoken of through the prophet Isaiah, who said:

A voice of one crying out in the wilderness:
Prepare the way for the Lord;
make his paths straight!

4 Now John had a camel-hair garment with a leather belt around his
waist, and his food was locusts and wild honey. 5 Then people from
Jerusalem, all Judea, and all the vicinity of the Jordan were going out
to him, 6 and they were baptized by him in the Jordan River, confessing
their sins.

7 When he saw many of the Pharisees and Sadducees coming to his
baptism, he said to them, "Brood of vipers! Who warned you to flee
from the coming wrath? 8 Therefore produce fruit consistent with
repentance. 9 And don't presume to say to yourselves, 'We have Abraham
as our father.' For I tell you that God is able to raise up children for
Abraham from these stones. 10 The ax is already at the root of the trees.
Therefore, every tree that doesn't produce good fruit will be cut down
and thrown into the fire.

11 "I baptize you with water for repentance, but the one who is coming
after me is more powerful than I. I am not worthy to remove his
sandals. He himself will baptize you with the Holy Spirit and fire. 12 His
winnowing shovel is in his hand, and he will clear his threshing floor
and gather his wheat into the barn. But the chaff he will burn with fire
that never goes out."

THE BAPTISM OF JESUS

13 Then Jesus came from Galilee to John at the Jordan, to be baptized by
him. 14 But John tried to stop him, saying, "I need to be baptized by you,
and yet you come to me?"

15 Jesus answered him, "Allow it for now, because this is the way for us to
fulfill all righteousness." Then John allowed him to be baptized.

16 When Jesus was baptized, he went up immediately from the water.
The heavens suddenly opened for him, and he saw the Spirit of God
descending like a dove and coming down on him. 17 And a voice from
heaven said, "This is my beloved Son, with whom I am well-pleased."

Matthew 4

NOTES

THE TEMPTATION OF JESUS

1 Then Jesus was led up by the Spirit into the wilderness to be tempted by
the devil. 2 After he had fasted forty days and forty nights, he was hungry.
3 Then the tempter approached him and said, "If you are the Son of God,
tell these stones to become bread."

4 He answered, "It is written: Man must not live on bread alone but on
every word that comes from the mouth of God."

5 Then the devil took him to the holy city, had him stand on the pinnacle
of the temple, 6 and said to him, "If you are the Son of God, throw
yourself down. For it is written:

He will give his angels orders concerning you,
and they will support you with their hands
so that you will not strike
your foot against a stone."

7 Jesus told him, "It is also written: Do not test the Lord your God."

8 Again, the devil took him to a very high mountain and showed him
all the kingdoms of the world and their splendor. 9 And he said to him,
"I will give you all these things if you will fall down and worship me."

10 Then Jesus told him, "Go away, Satan! For it is written: Worship the
Lord your God, and serve only him."

11 Then the devil left him, and angels came and began to serve him.

MINISTRY IN GALILEE

12 When he heard that John had been arrested, he withdrew into Galilee.
13 He left Nazareth and went to live in Capernaum by the sea, in the
region of Zebulun and Naphtali. 14 This was to fulfill what was spoken
through the prophet Isaiah:

15 Land of Zebulun and land of Naphtali,
along the road by the sea, beyond the Jordan,
Galilee of the Gentiles.
16 The people who live in darkness
have seen a great light,
and for those living in the land of the shadow of death,
a light has dawned.

NOTES

[17] From then on Jesus began to preach, "Repent, because the kingdom of heaven
has come near."

THE FIRST DISCIPLES

[18] As he was walking along the Sea of Galilee, he saw two brothers, Simon (who
is called Peter), and his brother Andrew. They were casting a net into the sea—for
they were fishermen. [19] "Follow me," he told them, "and I will make you fish for
people." [20] Immediately they left their nets and followed him.

[21] Going on from there, he saw two other brothers, James the son of Zebedee, and
his brother John. They were in a boat with Zebedee their father, preparing their
nets, and he called them. [22] Immediately they left the boat and their father and
followed him.

TEACHING, PREACHING, AND HEALING

[23] Now Jesus began to go all over Galilee, teaching in their synagogues, preaching
the good news of the kingdom, and healing every disease and sickness among the
people. [24] Then the news about him spread throughout Syria. So they brought to
him all those who were afflicted, those suffering from various diseases and intense
pains, the demon-possessed, the epileptics, and the paralytics. And he healed
them. [25] Large crowds followed him from Galilee, the Decapolis, Jerusalem, Judea,
and beyond the Jordan.

GOING DEEPER

Isaiah 40:1–5

GOD'S PEOPLE COMFORTED

[1] "Comfort, comfort my people,"
says your God.
[2] "Speak tenderly to Jerusalem,
and announce to her
that her time of hard service is over,
her iniquity has been pardoned,
and she has received from the LORD's hand
double for all her sins."

3 A voice of one crying out:

NOTES

Prepare the way of the Lord in the wilderness;
make a straight highway for our God in the desert.
4 Every valley will be lifted up,
and every mountain and hill will be leveled;
the uneven ground will become smooth
and the rough places, a plain.
5 And the glory of the Lord will appear,
and all humanity together will see it,
for the mouth of the Lord has spoken.

John 1:1–13

PROLOGUE

1 In the beginning was the Word, and the Word was with God, and the Word was
God. 2 He was with God in the beginning. 3 All things were created through him,
and apart from him not one thing was created that has been created. 4 In him was
life, and that life was the light of men. 5 That light shines in the darkness, and yet
the darkness did not overcome it.

6 There was a man sent from God whose name was John. 7 He came as a witness
to testify about the light, so that all might believe through him. 8 He was not the
light, but he came to testify about the light. 9 The true light that gives light to
everyone was coming into the world.

10 He was in the world, and the world was created through him, and yet the world
did not recognize him. 11 He came to his own, and his own people did not receive
him. 12 But to all who did receive him, he gave them the right to be children of
God, to those who believe in his name, 13 who were born, not of natural descent,
or of the will of the flesh, or of the will of man, but of God.

Day

JESUS *Preaches* *the* SERMON *on* *the* MOUNT

03

Matthew 5

THE SERMON ON THE MOUNT

1 When he saw the crowds, he went up on the mountain, and
after he sat down, his disciples came to him. 2 Then he began
to teach them, saying:

THE BEATITUDES

3 "Blessed are the poor in spirit,
for the kingdom of heaven is theirs.
4 Blessed are those who mourn,
for they will be comforted.
5 Blessed are the humble,
for they will inherit the earth.
6 Blessed are those who hunger and thirst for righteousness,
for they will be filled.
7 Blessed are the merciful,
for they will be shown mercy.
8 Blessed are the pure in heart,
for they will see God.
9 Blessed are the peacemakers,
for they will be called sons of God.
10 Blessed are those who are persecuted because
of righteousness,
for the kingdom of heaven is theirs.

11 "You are blessed when they insult you and persecute you
and falsely say every kind of evil against you because of
me. 12 Be glad and rejoice, because your reward is great in
heaven. For that is how they persecuted the prophets who
were before you.

BELIEVERS ARE SALT AND LIGHT

13 "You are the salt of the earth. But if the salt should lose
its taste, how can it be made salty? It's no longer good
for anything but to be thrown out and trampled under
people's feet.

14 "You are the light of the world. A city situated on a hill
cannot be hidden. 15 No one lights a lamp and puts it under
a basket, but rather on a lampstand, and it gives light for all
who are in the house. 16 In the same way, let your light shine
before others, so that they may see your good works and give
glory to your Father in heaven.

CHRIST FULFILLS THE LAW

17 "Don't think that I came to abolish
the Law or the Prophets.

I did not come to abolish but to fulfill. 18 For truly I tell
you, until heaven and earth pass away, not the smallest letter
or one stroke of a letter will pass away from the law until
all things are accomplished. 19 Therefore, whoever breaks
one of the least of these commands and teaches others to
do the same will be called least in the kingdom of heaven.
But whoever does and teaches these commands will be called

Continued

NOTES

great in the kingdom of heaven. [20] For I tell you, unless your righteousness surpasses
that of the scribes and Pharisees, you will never get into the kingdom of hcaven.

MURDER BEGINS IN THE HEART

[21] "You have heard that it was said to our ancestors, Do not murder, and whoever
murders will be subject to judgment. [22] But I tell you, everyone who is angry with
his brother or sister will be subject to judgment. Whoever insults his brother or
sister will be subject to the court. Whoever says, 'You fool!' will be subject to
hellfire. [23] So if you are offering your gift on the altar, and there you remember that
your brother or sister has something against you, [24] leave your gift there in front of
the altar. First go and be reconciled with your brother or sister, and then come and
offer your gift. [25] Reach a settlement quickly with your adversary while you're on
the way with him to the court, or your adversary will hand you over to the judge,
and the judge to the officer, and you will be thrown into prison. [26] Truly I tell you,
you will never get out of there until you have paid the last penny.

ADULTERY BEGINS IN THE HEART

[27] "You have heard that it was said, Do not commit adultery. [28] But I tell you,
everyone who looks at a woman lustfully has already committed adultery with her
in his heart. [29] If your right eye causes you to sin, gouge it out and throw it away.
For it is better that you lose one of the parts of your body than for your whole body
to be thrown into hell. [30] And if your right hand causes you to sin, cut it off and
throw it away. For it is better that you lose one of the parts of your body than for
your whole body to go into hell.

DIVORCE PRACTICES CENSURED

[31] "It was also said, Whoever divorces his wife must give her a written notice
of divorce. [32] But I tell you, everyone who divorces his wife, except in a case of
sexual immorality, causes her to commit adultery. And whoever marries a divorced
woman commits adultery.

TELL THE TRUTH

[33] "Again, you have heard that it was said to our ancestors, You must not break
your oath, but you must keep your oaths to the Lord. [34] But I tell you, don't take an
oath at all: either by heaven, because it is God's throne; [35] or by the earth, because
it is his footstool; or by Jerusalem, because it is the city of the great King. [36] Do
not swear by your head, because you cannot make a single hair white or black.
[37] But let your 'yes' mean 'yes,' and your 'no' mean 'no.' Anything more than this
is from the evil one.

GO THE SECOND MILE

38 "You have heard that it was said, An eye for an eye and a tooth for a tooth.
39 But I tell you, don't resist an evildoer. On the contrary, if anyone slaps you on
your right cheek, turn the other to him also. 40 As for the one who wants to sue you
and take away your shirt, let him have your coat as well. 41 And if anyone forces
you to go one mile, go with him two. 42 Give to the one who asks you, and don't
turn away from the one who wants to borrow from you.

LOVE YOUR ENEMIES

43 "You have heard that it was said, Love your neighbor and hate your enemy. 44 But
I tell you, love your enemies and pray for those who persecute you, 45 so that you
may be children of your Father in heaven. For he causes his sun to rise on the evil
and the good, and sends rain on the righteous and the unrighteous. 46 For if you
love those who love you, what reward will you have? Don't even the tax collectors
do the same? 47 And if you greet only your brothers and sisters, what are you doing
out of the ordinary? Don't even the Gentiles do the same? 48 Be perfect, therefore,
as your heavenly Father is perfect."

GOING DEEPER

Psalm 40:6–8

6 You do not delight in sacrifice and offering;
you open my ears to listen.
You do not ask for a whole burnt offering or a sin offering.
7 Then I said, "See, I have come;
in the scroll it is written about me.
8 I delight to do your will, my God,
and your instruction is deep within me."

Romans 8:1–4

THE LIFE-GIVING SPIRIT

1 Therefore, there is now no condemnation for those in Christ Jesus, 2 because
the law of the Spirit of life in Christ Jesus has set you free from the law of sin and
death. 3 For what the law could not do since it was weakened by the flesh, God
did. He condemned sin in the flesh by sending his own Son in the likeness of sinful
flesh as a sin offering, 4 in order that the law's requirement would be fulfilled in us
who do not walk according to the flesh but according to the Spirit.

NOTES

Matthew's Five DISCOURSES

In his Gospel, Matthew collects and presents Jesus's teachings through five extended sections, known as the five discourses. Each section shows the variety of teaching styles that Jesus utilized in His ministry, including parables, sermons, warnings, and more for the purpose of helping His followers better understand the ways of His kingdom and His mission they were called to carry out in His name.

The Basics *of the* Faith

MATTHEW 5–7

An overview of the Christian life and the work of Christ. This discourse, most commonly known as the Sermon on the Mount, discusses the essential aspects of ethics, conduct, and worship for the Christ-follower.

- The Beatitudes (5:1–12)
- The characteristics of kingdom righteousness (5:13–48)
- The practice of kingdom righteousness (6:1–7:12)
- Seeking the kingdom of heaven (7:13–29)

The Mission *of the* Church

MATTHEW 10

Instruction directed to Jesus's twelve disciples, preparing them to take the gospel out into the world.

- Commissioning for ministry (10:1–15)
- Anticipating various responses to that ministry (10:16–42)

The Kingdom *of* Heaven

MATTHEW 13

A collection of parables focused on imparting Christian wisdom while revealing what the kingdom of heaven will be like.

- The parable of the sower, told and explained (13:1–23)
- Other kingdom parables (13:24–52)
- Responses to Jesus's parables (13:53–58)

The Character *of the* Christian

MATTHEW 18

Parables and teaching focused on the community of faith and the character of those who follow Jesus.

- Humility (18:1–14)
- Forgiveness (18:15–35)

The End *of* All Things

MATTHEW 24–25

A section of teaching on the judgment that will soon come to the world and the mercy that is found in Christ alone. Given near the time of Jesus's crucifixion, it is referred to as the Olivet Discourse as it was likely delivered from the Mount of Olives.

- Prophecy about the coming kingdom (24:1–35)
- Call to readiness (24:36–25:30)
- The promise of coming judgment (25:31–46)

DAY 04

JESUS'S *Sermon on the* MOUNT CONTINUED

Matthew 6

HOW TO GIVE

1 “Be careful not to practice your righteousness in front of
others to be seen by them. Otherwise, you have no reward
with your Father in heaven. 2 So whenever you give to the
poor, don't sound a trumpet before you, as the hypocrites
do in the synagogues and on the streets, to be applauded by
people. Truly I tell you, they have their reward. 3 But when
you give to the poor, don't let your left hand know what your
right hand is doing, 4 so that your giving may be in secret.
And your Father who sees in secret will reward you.

HOW TO PRAY

5 “Whenever you pray, you must not be like the hypocrites,
because they love to pray standing in the synagogues and
on the street corners to be seen by people. Truly I tell you,
they have their reward. 6 But when you pray, go into your
private room, shut your door, and pray to your Father who
is in secret. And your Father who sees in secret will reward
you. 7 When you pray, don't babble like the Gentiles, since
they imagine they'll be heard for their many words. 8 Don't
be like them, because your Father knows the things you need
before you ask him.

THE LORD'S PRAYER

9 “Therefore, you should pray like this:

Our Father in heaven,
your name be honored as holy.
10 Your kingdom come.
Your will be done
on earth as it is in heaven.
11 Give us today our daily bread.
12 And forgive us our debts,
as we also have forgiven our debtors.
13 And do not bring us into temptation,
but deliver us from the evil one.

14 “For if you forgive others their offenses, your heavenly
Father will forgive you as well. 15 But if you don't forgive
others, your Father will not forgive your offenses.

HOW TO FAST

16 “Whenever you fast, don't be gloomy like the hypocrites.
For they disfigure their faces so that their fasting is obvious
to people. Truly I tell you, they have their reward. 17 But

when you fast, put oil on your head and wash your face, 18 so that your fasting isn't
obvious to others but to your Father who is in secret. And your Father who sees in
secret will reward you.

GOD AND POSSESSIONS

19 "Don't store up for yourselves treasures on earth, where moth and rust destroy
and where thieves break in and steal. 20 But store up for yourselves treasures in
heaven, where neither moth nor rust destroys, and where thieves don't break in and
steal. 21 For where your treasure is, there your heart will be also.

22 "The eye is the lamp of the body. If your eye is healthy, your whole body will be
full of light. 23 But if your eye is bad, your whole body will be full of darkness. So
if the light within you is darkness, how deep is that darkness!

24 "No one can serve two masters, since either he will hate one and love the other,
or he will be devoted to one and despise the other. You cannot serve both God
and money.

When you see this icon, use the prompts to make observations in the margin space about faith in the indicated passage. Your notes will help you answer the response questions on pages 64 and 128.

What images are used to describe faith and a lack of faith?

6:26–33

THE CURE FOR ANXIETY

25 "Therefore I tell you: Don't worry about your life, what you will eat or what you
will drink; or about your body, what you will wear. Isn't life more than food and
the body more than clothing? 26 Consider the birds of the sky: They don't sow or
reap or gather into barns, yet your heavenly Father feeds them. Aren't you worth
more than they? 27 Can any of you add one moment to his life span by worrying?
28 And why do you worry about clothes? Observe how the wildflowers of the field
grow: They don't labor or spin thread. 29 Yet I tell you that not even Solomon in all
his splendor was adorned like one of these. 30 If that's how God clothes the grass of
the field, which is here today and thrown into the furnace tomorrow, won't he do
much more for you—you of little faith? 31 So don't worry, saying, 'What will we
eat?' or 'What will we drink?' or 'What will we wear?' 32 For the Gentiles eagerly
seek all these things, and your heavenly Father knows that you need them. 33 But
seek first the kingdom of God and his righteousness, and all these things will be
provided for you.

34 Therefore don't worry about tomorrow,
because tomorrow will worry about itself.
Each day has enough trouble of its own."

Matthew 7

DO NOT JUDGE

1 "Do not judge, so that you won't be judged. 2 For you will be judged by the same
standard with which you judge others, and you will be measured by the same
measure you use. 3 Why do you look at the splinter in your brother's eye but don't

notice the beam of wood in your own eye? 4 Or how can you say to your brother, 'Let me take the splinter out of your eye,' and look, there's a beam of wood in your own eye? 5 Hypocrite! First take the beam of wood out of your eye, and then you will see clearly to take the splinter out of your brother's eye. 6 Don't give what is holy to dogs or toss your pearls before pigs, or they will trample them under their feet, turn, and tear you to pieces.

What images are used to describe faith and a lack of faith?

7:7–27

ASK, SEARCH, KNOCK

7 "Ask, and it will be given to you. Seek, and you will find. Knock, and the door will be opened to you. 8 For everyone who asks receives, and the one who seeks finds, and to the one who knocks, the door will be opened. 9 Who among you, if his son asks him for bread, will give him a stone? 10 Or if he asks for a fish, will give him a snake? 11 If you then, who are evil, know how to give good gifts to your children, how much more will your Father in heaven give good things to those who ask him. 12 Therefore, whatever you want others to do for you, do also the same for them, for this is the Law and the Prophets.

ENTERING THE KINGDOM

13 "Enter through the narrow gate. For the gate is wide and the road broad that leads to destruction, and there are many who go through it. 14 How narrow is the gate and difficult the road that leads to life, and few find it.

15 "Be on your guard against false prophets who come to you in sheep's clothing but inwardly are ravaging wolves. 16 You'll recognize them by their fruit. Are grapes gathered from thornbushes or figs from thistles? 17 In the same way, every good tree produces good fruit, but a bad tree produces bad fruit. 18 A good tree can't produce bad fruit; neither can a bad tree produce good fruit. 19 Every tree that doesn't produce good fruit is cut down and thrown into the fire. 20 So you'll recognize them by their fruit.

21 "Not everyone who says to me, 'Lord, Lord,' will enter the kingdom of heaven, but only the one who does the will of my Father in heaven. 22 On that day many will say to me, 'Lord, Lord, didn't we prophesy in your name, drive out demons in your name, and do many miracles in your name?' 23 Then I will announce to them, 'I never knew you. Depart from me, you lawbreakers!'

THE TWO FOUNDATIONS

24 "Therefore, everyone who hears these words of mine and acts on them will be like a wise man who built his house on the rock. 25 The rain fell, the rivers rose, and the winds blew and pounded that house. Yet it didn't collapse, because its foundation was on the rock. 26 But everyone who hears these words of mine and doesn't act on them will be like a foolish man who built his house on the sand. 27 The rain fell, the rivers rose, the winds blew and pounded that house, and it collapsed. It collapsed with a great crash."

28 When Jesus had finished saying these things, the crowds were astonished at his
teaching, 29 because he was teaching them like one who had authority, and not like
their scribes.

NOTES

GOING DEEPER

1 Chronicles 29:11–13

11 Yours, LORD, is the greatness and the power and the glory and the splendor and
the majesty, for everything in the heavens and on earth belongs to you. Yours,
LORD, is the kingdom, and you are exalted as head over all. 12 Riches and honor
come from you, and you are the ruler of everything. Power and might are in your
hand, and it is in your hand to make great and to give strength to all. 13 Now
therefore, our God, we give you thanks and praise your glorious name.

1 Timothy 6:6–12

6 But godliness with contentment is great gain. 7 For we brought nothing into
the world, and we can take nothing out. 8 If we have food and clothing, we will
be content with these. 9 But those who want to be rich fall into temptation, a
trap, and many foolish and harmful desires, which plunge people into ruin and
destruction. 10 For the love of money is a root of all kinds of evil, and by craving it,
some have wandered away from the faith and pierced themselves with many griefs.

FIGHT THE GOOD FIGHT

11 But you, man of God, flee from these things, and pursue righteousness,
godliness, faith, love, endurance, and gentleness. 12 Fight the good fight of the
faith. Take hold of eternal life to which you were called and about which you have
made a good confession in the presence of many witnesses.

Day 05

JESUS *Extends* *Healing* TO ALL

"I am willing; be made clean."

Matthew 8:3

Matthew 8

A MAN CLEANSED

1 When he came down from the mountain, large crowds followed him. 2 Right away a man with leprosy came up and knelt before him, saying,

"Lord, if you are willing, you can make me clean."

3 Reaching out his hand, Jesus touched him, saying, "I am willing; be made clean." Immediately his leprosy was cleansed. 4 Then Jesus told him, "See that you don't tell anyone; but go, show yourself to the priest, and offer the gift that Moses commanded, as a testimony to them."

A CENTURION'S FAITH

What occurred before and after Jesus commented on the centurion's faith? What actions does Jesus encourage?

8:5–13

5 When he entered Capernaum, a centurion came to him, pleading with him,
6 "Lord, my servant is lying at home paralyzed, in terrible agony."

7 He said to him, "Am I to come and heal him?"

8 "Lord," the centurion replied, "I am not worthy to have you come under my roof. But just say the word, and my servant will be healed. 9 For I too am a man under authority, having soldiers under my command. I say to this one, 'Go,' and he goes; and to another, 'Come,' and he comes; and to my servant, 'Do this!' and he does it."

10 Hearing this, Jesus was amazed and said to those following him, "Truly I tell you, I have not found anyone in Israel with so great a faith. 11 I tell you that many will come from east and west to share the banquet with Abraham, Isaac, and Jacob in the kingdom of heaven. 12 But the sons of the kingdom will be thrown into the outer darkness where there will be weeping and gnashing of teeth." 13 Then Jesus told the centurion, "Go. As you have believed, let it be done for you." And his servant was healed that very moment.

HEALINGS AT CAPERNAUM

14 Jesus went into Peter's house and saw his mother-in-law lying in bed with a fever. 15 So he touched her hand, and the fever left her. Then she got up and began to serve him. 16 When evening came, they brought to him many who were demon-possessed. He drove out the spirits with a word and healed all who were sick, 17 so that what was spoken through the prophet Isaiah might be fulfilled:

He himself took our weaknesses
and carried our diseases.

THE COST OF FOLLOWING JESUS

18 When Jesus saw a large crowd around him, he gave the order to go to the other side of the sea. 19 A scribe approached him and said, "Teacher, I will follow you wherever you go."

20 Jesus told him, "Foxes have dens, and birds of the sky have nests, but the Son of Man has no place to lay his head."

21 "Lord," another of his disciples said, "first let me go bury my father."

22 But Jesus told him, "Follow me, and let the dead bury their own dead."

WIND AND WAVES OBEY JESUS

23 As he got into the boat, his disciples followed him. 24 Suddenly, a violent storm arose on the sea, so that the boat was being swamped by the waves—but Jesus kept sleeping. 25 So the disciples came and woke him up, saying, "Lord, save us! We're going to die!"

What occurred before and after Jesus commented on the disciples' faith? What actions does Jesus encourage?

8:23–27

26 He said to them, "Why are you afraid, you of little faith?" Then he got up and rebuked the winds and the sea, and there was a great calm.

27 The men were amazed and asked, "What kind of man is this? Even the winds and the sea obey him!"

DEMONS DRIVEN OUT BY JESUS

28 When he had come to the other side, to the region of the Gadarenes, two demon-possessed men met him as they came out of the tombs. They were so violent that no one could pass that way. 29 Suddenly they shouted, "What do you have to do with us, Son of God? Have you come here to torment us before the time?"

30 A long way off from them, a large herd of pigs was feeding. 31 "If you drive us out," the demons begged him, "send us into the herd of pigs."

32 "Go!" he told them. So when they had come out, they entered the pigs, and the whole herd rushed down the steep bank into the sea and perished in the water. 33 Then the men who tended them fled. They went into the city and reported everything, especially what had happened to those who were demon-possessed. 34 At that, the whole town went out to meet Jesus. When they saw him, they begged him to leave their region.

GOING DEEPER

Psalm 103:1–5

THE FORGIVING GOD

Of David.

1 My soul, bless the Lord,
and all that is within me, bless his holy name.
2 My soul, bless the Lord,
and do not forget all his benefits.

3 He forgives all your iniquity;
he heals all your diseases.
4 He redeems your life from the Pit;
he crowns you with faithful love
and compassion.
5 He satisfies you with good things;
your youth is renewed like the eagle.

Acts 10:37–38

37 You know the events that took place throughout all Judea, beginning from Galilee after the baptism that John preached: 38 how God anointed Jesus of Nazareth with the Holy Spirit and with power, and how he went about doing good and healing all who were under the tyranny of the devil, because God was with him.

GRACE *Day*

DAY 06

Take this day to catch up on your reading, pray, and rest in the presence of the Lord.

Therefore, there is now no condemnation for those in Christ Jesus, because the law of the Spirit of life in Christ Jesus has set you free from the law of sin and death.

Romans 8:1–2

DAY
07

Weekly TRUTH

Scripture is God-breathed and true. When we memorize it, we carry the good news of Jesus with us wherever we go.

As we read the Gospel of Matthew, we will memorize our key verse, where Jesus proclaims the arrival of God's kingdom. This week we will start memorizing the first part of the verse.

From then on Jesus began to preach, "Repent, because the kingdom of heaven has come near."

Matthew 4:17

See tips for memorizing Scripture on page 132.

DAY 08

JESUS *Restores* *and* FORGIVES

"Have courage, daughter," he said. "Your faith has saved you."

Matthew 9:22

Matthew 9

NOTES

THE SON OF MAN FORGIVES AND HEALS

1 So he got into a boat, crossed over, and came to his own town. 2 Just then some
men brought to him a paralytic lying on a stretcher. Seeing their faith, Jesus told
the paralytic, "Have courage, son, your sins are forgiven."

3 At this, some of the scribes said to themselves, "He's blaspheming!"

4 Perceiving their thoughts, Jesus said, "Why are you thinking evil things in your
hearts? 5 For which is easier: to say, 'Your sins are forgiven,' or to say, 'Get up and
walk'? 6 But so that you may know that the Son of Man has authority on earth
to forgive sins"—then he told the paralytic, "Get up, take your stretcher, and go
home." 7 So he got up and went home. 8 When the crowds saw this, they were
awestruck and gave glory to God, who had given such authority to men.

THE CALL OF MATTHEW

9 As Jesus went on from there, he saw a man named Matthew sitting at the tax
office, and he said to him, "Follow me," and he got up and followed him.

10 While he was reclining at the table in the house, many tax collectors and sinners
came to eat with Jesus and his disciples. 11 When the Pharisees saw this, they asked
his disciples, "Why does your teacher eat with tax collectors and sinners?"

12 Now when he heard this, he said, "It is not those who are well who need a
doctor, but those who are sick. 13 Go and learn what this means: I desire mercy and
not sacrifice. For I didn't come to call the righteous, but sinners."

A QUESTION ABOUT FASTING

14 Then John's disciples came to him, saying, "Why do we and the Pharisees fast
often, but your disciples do not fast?"

15 Jesus said to them, "Can the wedding guests be sad while the groom is with
them? The time will come when the groom will be taken away from them, and
then they will fast. 16 No one patches an old garment with unshrunk cloth, because
the patch pulls away from the garment and makes the tear worse. 17 And no one
puts new wine into old wineskins. Otherwise, the skins burst, the wine spills out,
and the skins are ruined. No, they put new wine into fresh wineskins, and both
are preserved."

A GIRL RESTORED AND A WOMAN HEALED

18 As he was telling them these things, suddenly one of the leaders came and knelt
down before him, saying, "My daughter just died, but come and lay your hand
on her, and she will live." 19 So Jesus and his disciples got up and followed him.

What occurred before and after Jesus commented on the woman's faith? What actions does Jesus encourage?

9:20–31

20 Just then, a woman who had suffered from bleeding for twelve years approached from behind and touched the end of his robe, 21 for she said to herself, "If I can just touch his robe, I'll be made well."

22 Jesus turned and saw her. "Have courage, daughter," he said. "Your faith has saved you."

And the woman was made well from that moment.

23 When Jesus came to the leader's house, he saw the flute players and a crowd lamenting loudly. 24 "Leave," he said, "because the girl is not dead but asleep." And they laughed at him. 25 After the crowd had been put outside, he went in and took her by the hand, and the girl got up. 26 Then news of this spread throughout that whole area.

HEALING THE BLIND

27 As Jesus went on from there, two blind men followed him, calling out, "Have mercy on us, Son of David!"

28 When he entered the house, the blind men approached him, and Jesus said to them, "Do you believe that I can do this?"

They said to him, "Yes, Lord."

29 Then he touched their eyes, saying, "Let it be done for you according to your faith." 30 And their eyes were opened. Then Jesus warned them sternly, "Be sure that no one finds out." 31 But they went out and spread the news about him throughout that whole area.

DRIVING OUT A DEMON

32 Just as they were going out, a demon-possessed man who was unable to speak was brought to him. 33 When the demon had been driven out, the man who had been mute spoke, and the crowds were amazed, saying, "Nothing like this has ever been seen in Israel!"

34 But the Pharisees said, "He drives out demons by the ruler of the demons."

THE LORD OF THE HARVEST

35 Jesus continued going around to all the towns and villages, teaching in their synagogues, preaching the good news of the kingdom, and healing every disease and every sickness. 36 When he saw the crowds, he felt compassion for them, because they were distressed and dejected, like sheep without a shepherd. 37 Then he said to his disciples, "The harvest is abundant, but the workers are few. 38 Therefore, pray to the Lord of the harvest to send out workers into his harvest."

NOTES

Psalm 51:17

The sacrifice pleasing to God is a broken spirit.
You will not despise a broken and humbled heart, God.

Romans 5:1–5

FAITH TRIUMPHS

1 Therefore, since we have been justified by faith, we have peace with God through
our Lord Jesus Christ. 2 We have also obtained access through him by faith into
this grace in which we stand, and we boast in the hope of the glory of God. 3 And
not only that, but we also boast in our afflictions, because we know that affliction
produces endurance, 4 endurance produces proven character, and proven character
produces hope. 5 This hope will not disappoint us, because God's love has been
poured out in our hearts through the Holy Spirit who was given to us.

Day 09

JESUS *Sends* *the* TWELVE

Matthew 10

COMMISSIONING THE TWELVE

1 Summoning his twelve disciples, he gave them authority over
unclean spirits, to drive them out and to heal every disease
and sickness. 2 These are the names of the twelve apostles:
First, Simon, who is called Peter, and Andrew his brother;
James the son of Zebedee, and John his brother; 3 Philip and
Bartholomew; Thomas and Matthew the tax collector; James
the son of Alphaeus, and Thaddaeus; 4 Simon the Zealot, and
Judas Iscariot, who also betrayed him.

5 Jesus sent out these twelve after giving them instructions:
"Don't take the road that leads to the Gentiles, and don't
enter any Samaritan town. 6 Instead, go to the lost sheep of
the house of Israel. 7 As you go, proclaim, 'The kingdom of
heaven has come near.'

8 Heal the sick, raise the dead, cleanse those with leprosy, drive out demons. Freely you received, freely give.

9 Don't acquire gold, silver, or copper for your money-belts.
10 Don't take a traveling bag for the road, or an extra shirt,
sandals, or a staff, for the worker is worthy of his food.
11 When you enter any town or village, find out who is
worthy, and stay there until you leave. 12 Greet a household
when you enter it, 13 and if the household is worthy, let your
peace be on it; but if it is unworthy, let your peace return
to you. 14 If anyone does not welcome you or listen to your
words, shake the dust off your feet when you leave that house
or town. 15 Truly I tell you, it will be more tolerable on the
day of judgment for the land of Sodom and Gomorrah than
for that town.

PERSECUTIONS PREDICTED

16 "Look, I'm sending you out like sheep among wolves.
Therefore be as shrewd as serpents and as innocent as doves.
17 Beware of them, because they will hand you over to local
courts and flog you in their synagogues. 18 You will even be
brought before governors and kings because of me, to bear
witness to them and to the Gentiles. 19 But when they hand
you over, don't worry about how or what you are to speak.
For you will be given what to say at that hour, 20 because it
isn't you speaking, but the Spirit of your Father is speaking
through you.

21 "Brother will betray brother to death, and a father his
child. Children will rise up against parents and have them
put to death. 22 You will be hated by everyone because of my

Continued

NOTES

name. But the one who endures to the end will be saved. 23 When they persecute you in one town, flee to another. For truly I tell you, you will not have gone through the towns of Israel before the Son of Man comes. 24 A disciple is not above his teacher, or a slave above his master. 25 It is enough for a disciple to become like his teacher and a slave like his master. If they called the head of the house 'Beelzebul,' how much more the members of his household!

FEAR GOD

26 "Therefore, don't be afraid of them, since there is nothing covered that won't be uncovered and nothing hidden that won't be made known. 27 What I tell you in the dark, speak in the light. What you hear in a whisper, proclaim on the housetops. 28 Don't fear those who kill the body but are not able to kill the soul; rather, fear him who is able to destroy both soul and body in hell. 29 Aren't two sparrows sold for a penny? Yet not one of them falls to the ground without your Father's consent. 30 But even the hairs of your head have all been counted. 31 So don't be afraid; you are worth more than many sparrows.

ACKNOWLEDGING CHRIST

32 "Therefore, everyone who will acknowledge me before others, I will also acknowledge him before my Father in heaven. 33 But whoever denies me before others, I will also deny him before my Father in heaven. 34 Don't assume that I came to bring peace on the earth. I did not come to bring peace, but a sword. 35 For I came to turn

a man against his father,
a daughter against her mother,
a daughter-in-law against her mother-in-law;
36 and a man's enemies will be
the members of his household.

37 The one who loves a father or mother more than me is not worthy of me; the one who loves a son or daughter more than me is not worthy of me. 38 And whoever doesn't take up his cross and follow me is not worthy of me. 39 Anyone who finds his life will lose it, and anyone who loses his life because of me will find it.

A CUP OF COLD WATER

40 "The one who welcomes you welcomes me, and the one who welcomes me welcomes him who sent me. 41 Anyone who welcomes a prophet because he is a prophet will receive a prophet's reward. And anyone who welcomes a righteous person because he's righteous will receive a righteous person's reward. 42 And whoever gives even a cup of cold water to one of these little ones because he is a disciple, truly I tell you, he will never lose his reward."

GOING DEEPER

NOTES

Acts 1:13

When they arrived, they went to the room upstairs where they were staying: Peter, John, James, Andrew, Philip, Thomas, Bartholomew, Matthew, James the son of Alphaeus, Simon the Zealot, and Judas the son of James.

Ephesians 4:11–13

11 And he himself gave some to be apostles, some prophets, some evangelists, some
pastors and teachers, 12 to equip the saints for the work of ministry, to build up
the body of Christ, 13 until we all reach unity in the faith and in the knowledge
of God's Son, growing into maturity with a stature measured by Christ's fullness.

Jesus DAY 10 GIVES *Rest*

Matthew 11

JOHN THE BAPTIST DOUBTS

1 When Jesus had finished giving instructions to his twelve disciples, he moved on from there to teach and preach in their towns. 2 Now when John heard in prison what the Christ was doing, he sent a message through his disciples 3 and asked him, "Are you the one who is to come, or should we expect someone else?"

4 Jesus replied to them, "Go and report to John what you hear and see: 5 The blind receive their sight, the lame walk, those with leprosy are cleansed, the deaf hear, the dead are raised, and the poor are told the good news, 6 and blessed is the one who isn't offended by me."

7 As these men were leaving, Jesus began to speak to the crowds about John: "What did you go out into the wilderness to see? A reed swaying in the wind? 8 What then did you go out to see? A man dressed in soft clothes? See, those who wear soft clothes are in royal palaces. 9 What then did you go out to see? A prophet? Yes, I tell you, and more than a prophet. 10 This is the one about whom it is written:

> See, I am sending my messenger ahead of you;
> he will prepare your way before you.

11 "Truly I tell you, among those born of women no one greater than John the Baptist has appeared, but the least in the kingdom of heaven is greater than he. 12 From the days of John the Baptist until now, the kingdom of heaven has been suffering violence, and the violent have been seizing it by force. 13 For all the prophets and the law prophesied until John. 14 And if you're willing to accept it, he is the Elijah who is to come. 15 Let anyone who has ears listen.

AN UNRESPONSIVE GENERATION

16 "To what should I compare this generation? It's like children sitting in the marketplaces who call out to other children:

> 17 We played the flute for you,
> but you didn't dance;
> we sang a lament,
> but you didn't mourn!

NOTES

18 For John came neither eating nor drinking, and they say, 'He has a demon!'
19 The Son of Man came eating and drinking, and they say, 'Look, a glutton and
a drunkard, a friend of tax collectors and sinners!' Yet wisdom is vindicated by
her deeds."

20 Then he proceeded to denounce the towns where most of his miracles were done,
because they did not repent: 21 "Woe to you, Chorazin! Woe to you, Bethsaida!
For if the miracles that were done in you had been done in Tyre and Sidon, they
would have repented in sackcloth and ashes long ago. 22 But I tell you, it will be
more tolerable for Tyre and Sidon on the day of judgment than for you. 23 And
you, Capernaum, will you be exalted to heaven? No, you will go down to Hades.
For if the miracles that were done in you had been done in Sodom, it would have
remained until today. 24 But I tell you, it will be more tolerable for the land of
Sodom on the day of judgment than for you."

THE SON GIVES KNOWLEDGE AND REST

25 At that time Jesus said, "I praise you, Father, Lord of heaven and earth, because
you have hidden these things from the wise and intelligent and revealed them
to infants. 26 Yes, Father, because this was your good pleasure. 27 All things have
been entrusted to me by my Father. No one knows the Son except the Father, and
no one knows the Father except the Son and anyone to whom the Son desires to
reveal him.

28 "Come to me, all of you who are weary and burdened, and I will give you rest.
29 Take up my yoke and learn from me, because I am lowly and humble in heart,
and you will find rest for your souls.

30 For my yoke is easy and my burden is light."

GOING DEEPER

Psalm 23

THE GOOD SHEPHERD

A psalm of David.

1 The LORD is my shepherd;
I have what I need.
2 He lets me lie down in green pastures;
he leads me beside quiet waters.
3 He renews my life;
he leads me along the right paths
for his name's sake.

4 Even when I go through the darkest valley,
I fear no danger,
for you are with me;
your rod and your staff—they comfort me.

5 You prepare a table before me
in the presence of my enemies;
you anoint my head with oil;
my cup overflows.
6 Only goodness and faithful love will pursue me
all the days of my life,
and I will dwell in the house of the LORD
as long as I live.

John 15:1–11

THE VINE AND THE BRANCHES

1 "I am the true vine, and my Father is the gardener. 2 Every branch in me that does
not produce fruit he removes, and he prunes every branch that produces fruit so
that it will produce more fruit. 3 You are already clean because of the word I have
spoken to you. 4 Remain in me, and I in you. Just as a branch is unable to produce
fruit by itself unless it remains on the vine, neither can you unless you remain in
me. 5 I am the vine; you are the branches. The one who remains in me and I in him
produces much fruit, because you can do nothing without me. 6 If anyone does not
remain in me, he is thrown aside like a branch and he withers. They gather them,
throw them into the fire, and they are burned. 7 If you remain in me and my words
remain in you, ask whatever you want and it will be done for you. 8 My Father is
glorified by this: that you produce much fruit and prove to be my disciples.

CHRISTLIKE LOVE

9 "As the Father has loved me, I have also loved you. Remain in my love. 10 If you
keep my commands you will remain in my love, just as I have kept my Father's
commands and remain in his love.

11 "I have told you these things so that my joy may be in you and your joy may
be complete."

NOTES

DAY 11

JESUS *Is* LORD *of the* SABBATH

Matthew 12

LORD OF THE SABBATH

1 At that time Jesus passed through the grainfields on the Sabbath. His disciples were hungry and began to pick and eat some heads of grain. 2 When the Pharisees saw this, they said to him, "See, your disciples are doing what is not lawful to do on the Sabbath."

3 He said to them, "Haven't you read what David did when he and those who were with him were hungry: 4 how he entered the house of God, and they ate the bread of the Presence—which is not lawful for him or for those with him to eat, but only for the priests? 5 Or haven't you read in the law that on Sabbath days the priests in the temple violate the Sabbath and are innocent?

6 I tell you that something greater than the temple is here.

7 If you had known what this means, I desire mercy and not sacrifice, you would not have condemned the innocent. 8 For the Son of Man is Lord of the Sabbath."

THE MAN WITH THE SHRIVELED HAND

9 Moving on from there, he entered their synagogue. 10 There he saw a man who had a shriveled hand, and in order to accuse him they asked him, "Is it lawful to heal on the Sabbath?"

11 He replied to them, "Who among you, if he had a sheep that fell into a pit on the Sabbath, wouldn't take hold of it and lift it out? 12 A person is worth far more than a sheep; so it is lawful to do what is good on the Sabbath."

13 Then he told the man, "Stretch out your hand." So he stretched it out, and it was restored, as good as the other. 14 But the Pharisees went out and plotted against him, how they might kill him.

THE SERVANT OF THE LORD

15 Jesus was aware of this and withdrew. Large crowds followed him, and he healed them all. 16 He warned them not to make him known, 17 so that what was spoken through the prophet Isaiah might be fulfilled:

18 Here is my servant whom I have chosen,
my beloved in whom I delight;
I will put my Spirit on him,
and he will proclaim justice to the nations.
19 He will not argue or shout,
and no one will hear his voice in the streets.
20 He will not break a bruised reed,
and he will not put out a smoldering wick,
until he has led justice to victory.
21 The nations will put their hope in his name.

A HOUSE DIVIDED

22 Then a demon-possessed man who was blind and unable
to speak was brought to him. He healed him, so that the man
could both speak and see. 23 All the crowds were astounded
and said, "Could this be the Son of David?"

24 When the Pharisees heard this, they said, "This man drives
out demons only by Beelzebul, the ruler of the demons."

25 Knowing their thoughts, he told them, "Every kingdom
divided against itself is headed for destruction, and no city
or house divided against itself will stand. 26 If Satan drives
out Satan, he is divided against himself. How then will his
kingdom stand? 27 And if I drive out demons by Beelzebul,
by whom do your sons drive them out? For this reason
they will be your judges. 28 If I drive out demons by the
Spirit of God, then the kingdom of God has come upon
you. 29 How can someone enter a strong man's house and
steal his possessions unless he first ties up the strong man?
Then he can plunder his house. 30 Anyone who is not with
me is against me, and anyone who does not gather with me
scatters. 31 Therefore, I tell you, people will be forgiven every
sin and blasphemy, but the blasphemy against the Spirit will
not be forgiven. 32 Whoever speaks a word against the Son of
Man, it will be forgiven him; but whoever speaks against the
Holy Spirit, it will not be forgiven him, either in this age or
in the one to come.

A TREE AND ITS FRUIT

33 "Either make the tree good and its fruit will be good, or
make the tree bad and its fruit will be bad; for a tree is known
by its fruit. 34 Brood of vipers! How can you speak good
things when you are evil? For the mouth speaks from the
overflow of the heart. 35 A good person produces good things
from his storeroom of good, and an evil person produces evil
things from his storeroom of evil. 36 I tell you that on the day
of judgment people will have to account for every careless
word they speak. 37 For by your words you will be acquitted,
and by your words you will be condemned."

Continued

NOTES

THE SIGN OF JONAH

38 Then some of the scribes and Pharisees said to him, "Teacher, we want to see a sign from you."

39 He answered them, "An evil and adulterous generation demands a sign, but no sign will be given to it except the sign of the prophet Jonah. 40 For as Jonah was in the belly of the huge fish three days and three nights, so the Son of Man will be in the heart of the earth three days and three nights. 41 The men of Nineveh will stand up at the judgment with this generation and condemn it, because they repented at Jonah's preaching; and look—something greater than Jonah is here. 42 The queen of the south will rise up at the judgment with this generation and condemn it, because she came from the ends of the earth to hear the wisdom of Solomon; and look—something greater than Solomon is here.

AN UNCLEAN SPIRIT'S RETURN

43 "When an unclean spirit comes out of a person, it roams through waterless places looking for rest but doesn't find any. 44 Then it says, 'I'll go back to my house that I came from.' Returning, it finds the house vacant, swept, and put in order. 45 Then it goes and brings with it seven other spirits more evil than itself, and they enter and settle down there. As a result, that person's last condition is worse than the first. That's how it will also be with this evil generation."

TRUE RELATIONSHIPS

46 While he was still speaking with the crowds, his mother and brothers were standing outside wanting to speak to him. 47 Someone told him, "Look, your mother and your brothers are standing outside, wanting to speak to you."

48 He replied to the one who was speaking to him, "Who is my mother and who are my brothers?" 49 Stretching out his hand toward his disciples, he said, "Here are my mother and my brothers! 50 For whoever does the will of my Father in heaven is my brother and sister and mother."

NOTES

Genesis 2:3

God blessed the seventh day and declared it holy, for on it he rested from all his work of creation.

Acts 2:32–36

[32] God has raised this Jesus; we are all witnesses of this. [33] Therefore, since he
has been exalted to the right hand of God and has received from the Father the
promised Holy Spirit, he has poured out what you both see and hear. [34] For it was
not David who ascended into the heavens, but he himself says:

The Lord declared to my Lord,
"Sit at my right hand
[35] until I make your enemies your footstool."

[36] Therefore let all the house of Israel know with certainty that God has made this
Jesus, whom you crucified, both Lord and Messiah.

DAY 12

JESUS *Speaks* *in* PARABLES

"Let anyone who has ears listen."

MATTHEW 13:9

Matthew 13:1–52

THE PARABLE OF THE SOWER

1 On that day Jesus went out of the house and was sitting by the sea. 2 Such large crowds
gathered around him that he got into a boat and sat down, while the whole crowd stood
on the shore.

3 Then he told them many things in parables, saying, "Consider the sower who went out
to sow. 4 As he sowed, some seed fell along the path, and the birds came and devoured
them. 5 Other seed fell on rocky ground where it didn't have much soil, and it grew up
quickly since the soil wasn't deep. 6 But when the sun came up, it was scorched, and since
it had no root, it withered away. 7 Other seed fell among thorns, and the thorns came up
and choked it. 8 Still other seed fell on good ground and produced fruit: some a hundred,
some sixty, and some thirty times what was sown. 9 Let anyone who has ears listen."

What images are used to describe faith and a lack of faith?

13:3–9

WHY JESUS USED PARABLES

10 Then the disciples came up and asked him, "Why are you speaking to them in parables?"

11 He answered, "Because the secrets of the kingdom of heaven have been given for you to
know, but it has not been given to them. 12 For whoever has, more will be given to him,
and he will have more than enough; but whoever does not have, even what he has will be
taken away from him. 13 That is why I speak to them in parables, because looking they
do not see, and hearing they do not listen or understand. 14 Isaiah's prophecy is fulfilled
in them, which says:

> You will listen and listen,
> but never understand;
> you will look and look,
> but never perceive.
> 15 For this people's heart has grown callous;
> their ears are hard of hearing,
> and they have shut their eyes;
> otherwise they might see with their eyes,
> and hear with their ears, and
> understand with their hearts,
> and turn back—
> and I would heal them.

16 "Blessed are your eyes because they do see, and your ears because they do hear. 17 For
truly I tell you, many prophets and righteous people longed to see the things you see but
didn't see them, to hear the things you hear but didn't hear them.

THE PARABLE OF THE SOWER EXPLAINED

18 "So listen to the parable of the sower: 19 When anyone hears the word about the kingdom
and doesn't understand it, the evil one comes and snatches away what was sown in his

heart. This is the one sown along the path. 20 And the one sown on rocky ground—this is one who hears the word and immediately receives it with joy. 21 But he has no root and is short-lived. When distress or persecution comes because of the word, immediately he falls away. 22 Now the one sown among the thorns—this is one who hears the word, but the worries of this age and the deceitfulness of wealth choke the word, and it becomes unfruitful. 23 But the one sown on the good ground—this is one who hears and understands the word, who does produce fruit and yields: some a hundred, some sixty, some thirty times what was sown."

THE PARABLE OF THE WHEAT AND THE WEEDS

24 He presented another parable to them: "The kingdom of heaven may be compared to a man who sowed good seed in his field. 25 But while people were sleeping, his enemy came, sowed weeds among the wheat, and left. 26 When the plants sprouted and produced grain, then the weeds also appeared. 27 The landowner's servants came to him and said, 'Master, didn't you sow good seed in your field? Then where did the weeds come from?'

28 "'An enemy did this,' he told them.

"'So, do you want us to go and pull them up?' the servants asked him.

29 "'No,' he said. 'When you pull up the weeds, you might also uproot the wheat with them. 30 Let both grow together until the harvest. At harvest time I'll tell the reapers: Gather the weeds first and tie them in bundles to burn them, but collect the wheat in my barn.'"

THE PARABLES OF THE MUSTARD SEED AND OF THE LEAVEN

31 He presented another parable to them: "The kingdom of heaven is like a mustard seed that a man took and sowed in his field. 32 It's the smallest of all the seeds, but when grown, it's taller than the garden plants and becomes a tree, so that the birds of the sky come and nest in its branches."

33 He told them another parable: "The kingdom of heaven is like leaven that a woman took and mixed into fifty pounds of flour until all of it was leavened."

USING PARABLES FULFILLS PROPHECY

34 Jesus told the crowds all these things in parables, and he did not tell them anything without a parable, 35 so that what was spoken through the prophet might be fulfilled:

I will open my mouth in parables;
I will declare things kept secret
from the foundation of the world.

JESUS INTERPRETS THE PARABLE OF THE WHEAT AND THE WEEDS

36 Then he left the crowds and went into the house. His disciples approached him and said, "Explain to us the parable of the weeds in the field."

37 He replied, "The one who sows the good seed is the Son of Man; 38 the field is the world; and the good seed—these are the children of the kingdom. The weeds are the children of the evil one, 39 and the enemy who sowed them is the devil. The harvest is the end of the age, and the harvesters are angels. 40 Therefore, just as the weeds are gathered and burned in the fire, so it will be at the end of the age. 41 The Son of Man will send out his angels, and they will gather from his kingdom all who cause sin and those guilty of lawlessness. 42 They will throw them into the blazing furnace where there will be weeping and gnashing of teeth. 43 Then the righteous will shine like the sun in their Father's kingdom. Let anyone who has ears listen.

THE PARABLES OF THE HIDDEN TREASURE AND OF THE PRICELESS PEARL

44 "The kingdom of heaven is like treasure, buried in a field, that a man found and reburied. Then in his joy he goes and sells everything he has and buys that field.

45 "Again, the kingdom of heaven is like a merchant in search of fine pearls. 46 When he found one priceless pearl, he went and sold everything he had and bought it.

THE PARABLE OF THE NET

47 "Again, the kingdom of heaven is like a large net thrown into the sea. It collected every kind of fish, 48 and when it was full, they dragged it ashore, sat down, and gathered the good fish into containers, but threw out the worthless ones.

NOTES

[49] So it will be at the end of the age. The angels will go out, separate the evil people
from the righteous, [50] and throw them into the blazing furnace, where there will
be weeping and gnashing of teeth.

THE STOREHOUSE OF TRUTH

[51] "Have you understood all these things?"

They answered him, "Yes."

[52] "Therefore," he said to them, "every teacher of the law who has become a disciple in the kingdom of heaven is like the owner of a house who brings out of his storeroom treasures new and old."

GOING DEEPER

Psalm 78:1–4

LESSONS FROM ISRAEL'S PAST

A Maskil *of Asaph.*

[1] My people, hear my instruction;
listen to the words from my mouth.
[2] I will declare wise sayings;
I will speak mysteries from the past—
[3] things we have heard and known
and that our ancestors have passed down to us.
[4] We will not hide them from their children,
but will tell a future generation
the praiseworthy acts of the LORD,
his might, and the wondrous works
he has performed.

James 3:17–18

[17] But the wisdom from above is first pure, then peace-loving, gentle, compliant,
full of mercy and good fruits, unwavering, without pretense. [18] And the fruit of
righteousness is sown in peace by those who cultivate peace.

RESPOND

As we read through the book of Matthew, we're paying attention to the ways faith is described and how Jesus tells us to live in light of our belief.

Look back over your notes from the last two weeks. What patterns or consistent actions, images, or themes did you observe about how Jesus describes faith in action in His teaching and ministry?

01

What temptations, doubts, or distractions were obstacles to faith for the people in these stories?

02

What does your life look like when you act based on those obstacles to faith? What does your life look like when you act based on your faith in Christ?

03

GRACE *Day*

DAY
13

Take this day to catch up on your reading, pray, and rest in the presence of the Lord.

The LORD is my shepherd;
I have what I need.

Psalm 23:1

DAY
14

Weekly TRUTH

Scripture is God-breathed and true. When we memorize it, we carry the good news of Jesus with us wherever we go.

This week, we will memorize the last part of our key verse—Jesus's message of repentance and salvation.

From then on Jesus began to preach, "Repent, because the kingdom of heaven has come near."

Matthew 4:17

See tips for memorizing Scripture on page 132.

Day 15

JESUS *Is the* SON *of* GOD

"Have courage! It is I. Don't be afraid."

Matthew 14:27

Matthew 13:53–58

REJECTION AT NAZARETH

53 When Jesus had finished these parables, he left there. 54 He went to his hometown and began to teach them in their synagogue, so that they were astonished and said, "Where did this man get this wisdom and these miraculous powers? 55 Isn't this the carpenter's son? Isn't his mother called Mary, and his brothers James, Joseph, Simon, and Judas? 56 And his sisters, aren't they all with us? So where does he get all these things?" 57 And they were offended by him.

Jesus said to them, "A prophet is not without honor except in his hometown and in his household." 58 And he did not do many miracles there because of their unbelief.

Matthew 14

JOHN THE BAPTIST BEHEADED

1 At that time Herod the tetrarch heard the report about Jesus. 2 "This is John the Baptist," he told his servants. "He has been raised from the dead, and that's why miraculous powers are at work in him."

3 For Herod had arrested John, chained him, and put him in prison on account of Herodias, his brother Philip's wife, 4 since John had been telling him, "It's not lawful for you to have her." 5 Though Herod wanted to kill John, he feared the crowd since they regarded John as a prophet.

6 When Herod's birthday celebration came, Herodias's daughter danced before them and pleased Herod. 7 So he promised with an oath to give her whatever she asked. 8 Prompted by her mother, she answered, "Give me John the Baptist's head here on a platter." 9 Although the king regretted it, he commanded that it be granted because of his oaths and his guests. 10 So he sent orders and had John beheaded in the prison. 11 His head was brought on a platter and given to the girl, who carried it to her mother. 12 Then his disciples came, removed the corpse, buried it, and went and reported to Jesus.

FEEDING OF THE FIVE THOUSAND

13 When Jesus heard about it, he withdrew from there by boat to a remote place to be alone. When the crowds heard this, they followed him on foot from the towns. 14 When he went ashore, he saw a large crowd, had compassion on them, and healed their sick.

15 When evening came, the disciples approached him and said, "This place is deserted, and it is already late. Send the crowds away so that they can go into the villages and buy food for themselves."

16 "They don't need to go away," Jesus told them. "You give them something to eat."

17 "But we only have five loaves and two fish here," they said to him.

18 "Bring them here to me," he said. 19 Then he commanded the crowds to sit down on the grass. He took the five loaves and the two fish, and looking up to heaven, he blessed them. He broke the loaves and gave them to the disciples, and the disciples gave them to the crowds. 20 Everyone ate and was satisfied. They picked up twelve baskets full of leftover pieces. 21 Now those who ate were about five thousand men, besides women and children.

WALKING ON THE WATER

22 Immediately he made the disciples get into the boat and go ahead of him to the other side, while he dismissed the crowds. 23 After dismissing the crowds, he went up on the mountain by himself to pray. Well into the night, he was there alone. 24 Meanwhile, the boat was already some distance from land, battered by the waves, because the wind was against them. 25 Jesus came toward them

What occurred before and after Jesus commented on the disciples' faith? What actions does Jesus encourage?

14:22–32

walking on the sea very early in the morning. [26] When the disciples saw him walking on the sea, they were terrified. "It's a ghost!" they said, and they cried out in fear.

[27] Immediately Jesus spoke to them. "Have courage! It is I. Don't be afraid."

[28] "Lord, if it's you," Peter answered him, "command me to come to you on the water."

[29] He said, "Come."

And climbing out of the boat, Peter started walking on
the water and came toward Jesus. [30] But when he saw the
strength of the wind, he was afraid, and beginning to sink he cried out, "Lord, save me!"

[31] Immediately Jesus reached out his hand, caught hold of him, and said to him, "You of little faith, why did you doubt?"

[32] When they got into the boat, the wind ceased. [33] Then
those in the boat worshiped him and said, "Truly you are the Son of God."

MIRACULOUS HEALINGS

[34] When they had crossed over, they came to shore at
Gennesaret. [35] When the men of that place recognized him,
they alerted the whole vicinity and brought to him all who
were sick. [36] They begged him that they might only touch
the end of his robe, and as many as touched it were healed.

GOING DEEPER

Isaiah 41:10

"Do not fear, for I am with you;
do not be afraid, for I am your God.
I will strengthen you; I will help you;
I will hold on to you with my righteous right hand."

1 John 5:1–6

[1] Everyone who believes that Jesus is the Christ has been
born of God, and everyone who loves the Father also loves
the one born of him. [2] This is how we know that we love
God's children: when we love God and obey his commands.
[3] For this is what love for God is: to keep his commands. And
his commands are not a burden, [4] because everyone who has
been born of God conquers the world. This is the victory that has conquered the world: our faith.

THE CERTAINTY OF GOD'S TESTIMONY

[5] Who is the one who conquers the world but the one who
believes that Jesus is the Son of God? [6] Jesus Christ—he is
the one who came by water and blood, not by water only, but by water and by blood. And the Spirit is the one who testifies, because the Spirit is the truth.

JESUS *Is* *the* MESSIAH

DAY 16

Matthew 15

THE TRADITION OF THE ELDERS

1 Then Jesus was approached by Pharisees and scribes from Jerusalem, who
asked, 2 "Why do your disciples break the tradition of the elders? For they
don't wash their hands when they eat."

3 He answered them, "Why do you break God's commandment because
of your tradition? 4 For God said: Honor your father and your mother;
and, Whoever speaks evil of father or mother must be put to death. 5 But
you say, 'Whoever tells his father or mother, "Whatever benefit you might
have received from me is a gift committed to the temple," 6 he does not
have to honor his father.' In this way, you have nullified the word of God
because of your tradition. 7 Hypocrites! Isaiah prophesied correctly about
you when he said:

> 8 This people honors me with their lips,
> but their heart is far from me.
> 9 They worship me in vain,
> teaching as doctrines human commands."

DEFILEMENT IS FROM WITHIN

10 Summoning the crowd, he told them, "Listen and understand: 11 It's not
what goes into the mouth that defiles a person, but what comes out of the
mouth—this defiles a person."

12 Then the disciples came up and told him, "Do you know that the
Pharisees took offense when they heard what you said?"

13 He replied, "Every plant that my heavenly Father didn't plant will be
uprooted. 14 Leave them alone! They are blind guides. And if the blind
guide the blind, both will fall into a pit."

15 Then Peter said, "Explain this parable to us."

16 "Do you still lack understanding?" he asked. 17 "Don't you realize that
whatever goes into the mouth passes into the stomach and is eliminated?
18 But what comes out of the mouth comes from the heart, and this defiles
a person. 19 For from the heart come evil thoughts, murders, adulteries,
sexual immoralities, thefts, false testimonies, slander. 20 These are the
things that defile a person; but eating with unwashed hands does not
defile a person."

A GENTILE MOTHER'S FAITH

[21] When Jesus left there, he withdrew to the area of Tyre and Sidon. [22] Just then a
Canaanite woman from that region came and kept crying out, "Have mercy on
me, Lord, Son of David! My daughter is severely tormented by a demon."

[23] Jesus did not say a word to her. His disciples approached him and urged him, "Send her away because she's crying out after us."

[24] He replied, "I was sent only to the lost sheep of the house of Israel."

[25] But she came, knelt before him, and said, "Lord, help me!"

[26] He answered, "It isn't right to take the children's bread and throw it to the dogs."

[27] "Yes, Lord," she said, "yet even the dogs eat the crumbs that fall from their masters' table."

[28] Then Jesus replied to her, "Woman, your faith is great. Let it be done for you as you want." And from that moment her daughter was healed.

What occurred before and after Jesus commented on the woman's faith? What actions does Jesus encourage?

15:21–28

HEALING MANY PEOPLE

[29] Moving on from there, Jesus passed along the Sea of Galilee. He went up on a
mountain and sat there, [30] and large crowds came to him, including the lame, the
blind, the crippled, those unable to speak, and many others. They put them at his
feet, and he healed them. [31] So the crowd was amazed when they saw those unable
to speak talking, the crippled restored, the lame walking, and the blind seeing, and
they gave glory to the God of Israel.

FEEDING OF THE FOUR THOUSAND

[32] Jesus called his disciples and said, "I have compassion on the crowd, because they've already stayed with me three days and have nothing to eat. I don't want to send them away hungry, otherwise they might collapse on the way."

[33] The disciples said to him, "Where could we get enough bread in this desolate place to feed such a crowd?"

[34] "How many loaves do you have?" Jesus asked them.

"Seven," they said, "and a few small fish."

NOTES

35 After commanding the crowd to sit down on the ground, 36 he took the seven loaves and the fish, gave thanks, broke them, and gave them to the disciples, and the disciples gave them to the crowds. 37 They all ate and were satisfied. They collected the leftover pieces—seven large baskets full. 38 Now there were four thousand men who had eaten, besides women and children. 39 After dismissing the crowds, he got into the boat and went to the region of Magadan.

Matthew 16

THE LEAVEN OF THE PHARISEES AND THE SADDUCEES

1 The Pharisees and Sadducees approached, and tested him, asking him to show them a sign from heaven. 2 He replied, "When evening comes you say, 'It will be good weather because the sky is red.' 3 And in the morning, 'Today will be stormy because the sky is red and threatening.' You know how to read the appearance of the sky, but you can't read the signs of the times. 4 An evil and adulterous generation demands a sign, but no sign will be given to it except the sign of Jonah." Then he left them and went away.

5 The disciples reached the other shore, and they had forgotten to take bread. 6 Then Jesus told them, "Watch out and beware of the leaven of the Pharisees and Sadducees."

7 They were discussing among themselves, "We didn't bring any bread."

8 Aware of this, Jesus said, "You of little faith, why are you discussing among yourselves that you do not have bread? 9 Don't you understand yet? Don't you remember the five loaves for the five thousand and how many baskets you collected? 10 Or the seven loaves for the four thousand and how many large baskets you collected? 11 Why is it you don't understand that when I told you, 'Beware of the leaven of the Pharisees and Sadducees,' it wasn't about bread?" 12 Then they understood that he had not told them to beware of the leaven in bread, but of the teaching of the Pharisees and Sadducees.

PETER'S CONFESSION OF THE MESSIAH

13 When Jesus came to the region of Caesarea Philippi, he asked his disciples,

"Who do people say that the Son of Man is?"

14 They replied, "Some say John the Baptist; others, Elijah; still others, Jeremiah or one of the prophets."

15 "But you," he asked them, "who do you say that I am?"

16 Simon Peter answered, "You are the Messiah, the Son of the living God."

17 Jesus responded, "Blessed are you, Simon son of Jonah, because flesh and blood
did not reveal this to you, but my Father in heaven. 18 And I also say to you that
you are Peter, and on this rock I will build my church, and the gates of Hades
will not overpower it. 19 I will give you the keys of the kingdom of heaven, and
whatever you bind on earth will have been bound in heaven, and whatever you
loose on earth will have been loosed in heaven." 20 Then he gave the disciples orders
to tell no one that he was the Messiah.

NOTES

HIS DEATH AND RESURRECTION PREDICTED

21 From then on Jesus began to point out to his disciples that it was necessary for
him to go to Jerusalem and suffer many things from the elders, chief priests, and
scribes, be killed, and be raised the third day. 22 Peter took him aside and began to
rebuke him, "Oh no, Lord! This will never happen to you!"

23 Jesus turned and told Peter, "Get behind me, Satan! You are a hindrance to me
because you're not thinking about God's concerns but human concerns."

TAKE UP YOUR CROSS

24 Then Jesus said to his disciples, "If anyone wants to follow after me, let him
deny himself, take up his cross, and follow me. 25 For whoever wants to save his life
will lose it, but whoever loses his life because of me will find it. 26 For what will it
benefit someone if he gains the whole world yet loses his life? Or what will anyone
give in exchange for his life? 27 For the Son of Man is going to come with his angels
in the glory of his Father, and then he will reward each according to what he has
done. 28 Truly I tell you, there are some standing here who will not taste death until
they see the Son of Man coming in his kingdom."

GOING DEEPER

Isaiah 28:16

Therefore the Lord God said:
"Look, I have laid a stone in Zion,
a tested stone,
a precious cornerstone, a sure foundation;
the one who believes will be unshakable."

Romans 10:9–11

9 If you confess with your mouth, "Jesus is Lord," and believe in your heart
that God raised him from the dead, you will be saved. 10 One believes with the
heart, resulting in righteousness, and one confesses with the mouth, resulting in
salvation. 11 For the Scripture says, Everyone who believes on him will not be put
to shame...

KEY

- Question
- Teaching
- Rebuke

HOW *Jesus* RESPONDS *to* QUESTIONS

Throughout His ministry, Jesus was asked to address many questions by His followers and opponents alike. However, there were a variety of intentions motivating each person, and Jesus responded to questions addressing these motives (Mt 12:25). This chart summarizes many of the questions recorded in Matthew's Gospel and Jesus's response.

WHO ASKS	QUESTION	RESPONSE
Disciples	Where could we get enough bread in this desolate place to feed such a crowd? **Mt 15:33**	
Chief priests and scribes	Do you hear what these children are saying? **Mt 21:16**	
Chief priests and elders	By what authority are you doing these things? Who gave you this authority? **Mt 21:23**	
John the Baptist	I need to be baptized by you, and yet you come to me? **Mt 3:14**	
John the Baptist	Are you the one who is to come, or should we expect someone else? **Mt 11:3**	
Disciples	Why are you speaking to them in parables? **Mt 13:10**	
Disciples	Do you know that the Pharisees took offense when they heard what you said? **Mt 15:12**	
Disciples	Why then do the scribes say that Elijah must come first? **Mt 17:10**	
Disciples	Why couldn't we drive it out? **Mt 17:19**	
Disciples	So who is greatest in the kingdom of heaven? **Mt 18:1**	
Peter	Lord, how many times must I forgive my brother or sister who sins against me? As many as seven times? **Mt 18:21**	

Continued

WHO ASKS	QUESTION	RESPONSE
Disciples	Then who can be saved? **Mt 19:25**	
Peter	So what will there be for us? **Mt 19:27**	
Disciples	How did the fig tree wither so quickly? **Mt 21:20**	
Sadducees	In the resurrection, then, whose wife will she be of the seven? **Mt 22:28**	
Pharisees	Teacher, which command in the law is the greatest? **Mt 22:36**	
Disciples	Tell us, when will these things happen? And what is the sign of your coming and of the end of the age? **Mt 24:3**	
Disciples	Surely not I, Lord? **Mt 26:17**	
Judas	Surely not I, Rabbi? **Mt 26:25**	
Demons	What do you have to do with us, Son of God? Have you come here to torment us before the time? **Mt 8:29**	
Pharisees and Sadducees	The Pharisees and Sadducees approached, and tested him, asking him to show them a sign from heaven. **Mt 16:1**	
John's disciples	Why do we and the Pharisees fast often, but your disciples do not fast? **Mt 9:14**	
Pharisees	Is it lawful to heal on the Sabbath? **Mt 12:10**	
Pharisees	Is it lawful for a man to divorce his wife on any grounds?...Why then...did Moses command us to give divorce papers and to send her away? **Mt 19:3, 7**	

Young ruler	Teacher, what good must I do to have eternal life?...Which ones?...What do I still lack? **Mt 19:16, 18, 20**	
Disciples	Why this waste? **Mt 26:8**	
Pharisees	Why do your disciples break the tradition of the elders? For they don't wash their hands when they eat. **Mt 15:2**	
Pharisees	Is it lawful to pay taxes to Caesar or not? **Mt 22:17**	

There is a noticeable change in how Jesus responded to questions as He moved toward the cross. During His trials before the Sanhedrin and Pilate, Jesus was asked a few questions.

WHO ASKS	QUESTION	RESPONSE
High priest	Don't you have an answer to what these men are testifying against you? **Mt 26:62**	Silence
Sanhedrin	Prophesy to us, Messiah! Who was it that hit you? **Mt 26:68**	No response recorded
Pilate	Are you the king of the Jews? **Mt 27:11**	"You say so."
Pilate	Don't you hear how much they are testifying against you? **Mt 27:13**	Silence

Day

JESUS'S *Glory and* POWER

17

Matthew 17

THE TRANSFIGURATION

[1] After six days Jesus took Peter, James, and his brother John and led them up on a high mountain by themselves. [2] He was transfigured in front of them, and his face shone like the sun; his clothes became as white as the light. [3] Suddenly, Moses and Elijah appeared to them, talking with him. [4] Then Peter said to Jesus, "Lord, it's good for us to be here. If you want, I will set up three shelters here: one for you, one for Moses, and one for Elijah."

[5] While he was still speaking, suddenly a bright cloud covered them, and a voice from the cloud said, "This is my beloved Son, with whom I am well-pleased. Listen to him!" [6] When the disciples heard this, they fell facedown and were terrified.

[7] Jesus came up, touched them, and said, "Get up; don't be afraid." [8] When they looked up they saw no one except Jesus alone.

[9] As they were coming down the mountain, Jesus commanded them, "Don't tell anyone about the vision until the Son of Man is raised from the dead."

[10] So the disciples asked him, "Why then do the scribes say that Elijah must come first?"

[11] "Elijah is coming and will restore everything," he replied. [12] "But I tell you: Elijah has already come, and they didn't recognize him. On the contrary, they did whatever they pleased to him. In the same way the Son of Man is going to suffer at their hands." [13] Then the disciples understood that he had spoken to them about John the Baptist.

THE POWER OF JESUS OVER A DEMON

[14] When they reached the crowd, a man approached and knelt down before him. [15] "Lord," he said, "have mercy on my son, because he has seizures and suffers terribly. He often falls into the fire and often into the water. [16] I brought him to your disciples, but they couldn't heal him."

[17] Jesus replied, "You unbelieving and perverse generation, how long will I be with you? How long must I put up with you? Bring him here to me." [18] Then Jesus rebuked the demon, and it came out of him, and from that moment the boy was healed.

[19] Then the disciples approached Jesus privately and said, "Why couldn't we drive it out?"

[20] "Because of your little faith," he told them. "For truly I tell you, if you have faith the size of a mustard seed, you will tell this mountain, 'Move from here to there,' and it will move. Nothing will be impossible for you."

What occurred before and after Jesus commented on faith in this passage? What actions does Jesus encourage?

17:14–20

THE SECOND PREDICTION OF HIS DEATH

22 As they were gathering together in Galilee, Jesus told them, "The Son of Man is about to be betrayed into the hands of men. 23 They will kill him, and on the third day he will be raised up." And they were deeply distressed.

PAYING THE TEMPLE TAX

24 When they came to Capernaum, those who collected the temple tax approached Peter and said, "Doesn't your teacher pay the temple tax?"

25 "Yes," he said.

When he went into the house, Jesus spoke to him first, "What do you think, Simon? From whom do earthly kings collect tariffs or taxes? From their sons or from strangers?"

26 "From strangers," he said.

"Then the sons are free," Jesus told him. 27 "But, so we won't offend them, go to the sea, cast in a fishhook, and take the first fish that you catch. When you open its mouth you'll find a coin. Take it and give it to them for me and you."

Matthew 18

WHO IS THE GREATEST?

1 At that time the disciples came to Jesus and asked, "So who is greatest in the kingdom of heaven?" 2 He called a small child and had him stand among them. 3 "Truly I tell you," he said, "unless you turn and become like little children, you will never enter the kingdom of heaven. 4 Therefore, whoever humbles himself like this child—this one is the greatest in the kingdom of heaven. 5 And whoever welcomes one child like this in my name welcomes me.

6 "But whoever causes one of these little ones who believe in me to fall away—it would be better for him if a heavy millstone were hung around his neck and he were drowned in the depths of the sea. 7 Woe to the world because of offenses. For offenses will inevitably come, but woe to that person by whom the offense comes. 8 If your hand or your foot causes you to fall away, cut it off and throw it away. It is better for you to enter life maimed or lame than to have two hands or two feet and be thrown into the eternal fire. 9 And if your eye causes you to fall away, gouge it out and throw it away. It is better for you to enter life with one eye than to have two eyes and be thrown into hellfire.

THE PARABLE OF THE LOST SHEEP

10 "See to it that you don't despise one of these little ones, because I tell you that in heaven their angels continually view the face of my Father in heaven. 12 What do you think? If someone has a hundred sheep, and one of them goes astray, won't he leave the ninety-nine on the hillside and go and search for the stray? 13 And if he finds it, truly I tell you, he rejoices over that sheep more than over the ninety-nine that did not go astray. 14 In the same way, it is not the will of your Father in heaven that one of these little ones perish.

RESTORING A BROTHER

15 "If your brother sins against you, go tell him his fault, between you and him alone. If he listens to you, you have won your brother. 16 But if he won't listen, take one or two others with you, so that by the testimony of two or three witnesses every fact may be established. 17 If he doesn't pay attention to them, tell the church. If he doesn't pay attention even to the church, let him be like a Gentile and a tax collector to you. 18 Truly I tell you, whatever you bind on earth will have been bound in heaven, and whatever you loose on earth will have been loosed in heaven. 19 Again, truly I tell you, if two of you on earth agree about any matter that you pray for, it will be done for you by my Father in heaven. 20 For where two or three are gathered together in my name, I am there among them."

THE PARABLE OF THE UNFORGIVING SERVANT

21 Then Peter approached him and asked, "Lord, how many times must I forgive my brother or sister who sins against me? As many as seven times?"

22 "I tell you, not as many as seven," Jesus replied, "but seventy times seven.

23 "For this reason, the kingdom of heaven can be compared to a king who wanted to settle accounts with his servants. 24 When he began to settle accounts, one who owed ten

thousand talents was brought before him. 25 Since he did not
have the money to pay it back, his master commanded that
he, his wife, his children, and everything he had be sold to
pay the debt.

26 "At this, the servant fell facedown before him and said, 'Be
patient with me, and I will pay you everything.' 27 Then the
master of that servant had compassion, released him, and
forgave him the loan.

28 "That servant went out and found one of his fellow
servants who owed him a hundred denarii. He grabbed him,
started choking him, and said, 'Pay what you owe!'

29 "At this, his fellow servant fell down and began begging
him, 'Be patient with me, and I will pay you back.' 30 But
he wasn't willing. Instead, he went and threw him into
prison until he could pay what was owed. 31 When the
other servants saw what had taken place, they were deeply
distressed and went and reported to their master everything
that had happened. 32 Then, after he had summoned him,
his master said to him, 'You wicked servant! I forgave you all
that debt because you begged me. 33 Shouldn't you also have
had mercy on your fellow servant, as I had mercy on you?'
34 And because he was angry, his master handed him over
to the jailers to be tortured until he could pay everything
that was owed. 35 So also my heavenly Father will do to you
unless every one of you forgives his brother or sister from
your heart."

GOING DEEPER

1 Kings 8:10–13

10 When the priests came out of the holy place, the cloud
filled the LORD's temple, 11 and because of the cloud, the
priests were not able to continue ministering, for the glory
of the LORD filled the temple.

12 Then Solomon said:

The LORD said that he would dwell in total darkness.
13 I have indeed built an exalted temple for you,
a place for your dwelling forever.

2 Peter 1:16–18

THE TRUSTWORTHY PROPHETIC WORD

16 For we did not follow cleverly contrived myths when we
made known to you the power and coming of our Lord Jesus
Christ; instead, we were eyewitnesses of his majesty. 17 For
he received honor and glory from God the Father when the
voice came to him from the Majestic Glory, saying "This
is my beloved Son, with whom I am well-pleased!" 18 We
ourselves heard this voice when it came from heaven while
we were with him on the holy mountain.

DAY 18

JESUS *Came* *to* SERVE

"The Son of Man did not come to be served,
but to serve, and to give his life as a ransom for many."

Matthew 20:28

Matthew 19

THE QUESTION OF DIVORCE

1 When Jesus had finished saying these things, he departed from Galilee and went to the region of Judea across the Jordan. 2 Large crowds followed him, and he healed them there. 3 Some Pharisees approached him to test him. They asked, "Is it lawful for a man to divorce his wife on any grounds?"

4 "Haven't you read," he replied, "that he who created them in the beginning made them male and female, 5 and he also said, 'For this reason a man will leave his father and mother and be joined to his wife, and the two will become one flesh'? 6 So they are no longer two, but one flesh. Therefore, what God has joined together, let no one separate."

7 "Why then," they asked him, "did Moses command us to give divorce papers and to send her away?"

8 He told them, "Moses permitted you to divorce your wives because of the hardness of your hearts, but it was not like that from the beginning. 9 I tell you, whoever divorces his wife, except for sexual immorality, and marries another commits adultery."

10 His disciples said to him, "If the relationship of a man with his wife is like this, it's better not to marry."

11 He responded, "Not everyone can accept this saying, but only those to whom it has been given. 12 For there are eunuchs who were born that way from their mother's womb, there are eunuchs who were made by men, and there are eunuchs who have made themselves that way because of the kingdom of heaven. The one who is able to accept it should accept it."

BLESSING THE CHILDREN

13 Then little children were brought to Jesus for him to place his hands on them and pray, but the disciples rebuked them. 14 Jesus said, "Leave the little children alone, and don't try to keep them from coming to me, because the kingdom of heaven belongs to such as these." 15 After placing his hands on them, he went on from there.

THE RICH YOUNG RULER

16 Just then someone came up and asked him, "Teacher, what good must I do to have eternal life?"

17 "Why do you ask me about what is good?" he said to him. "There is only one who is good. If you want to enter into life, keep the commandments."

18 "Which ones?" he asked him.

Jesus answered: Do not murder; do not commit adultery; do not steal; do not bear false witness; 19 honor your father and your mother; and love your neighbor as yourself.

20 "I have kept all these," the young man told him. "What do I still lack?"

21 "If you want to be perfect," Jesus said to him, "go, sell your belongings and give to the poor, and you will have treasure in heaven. Then come, follow me."

22 When the young man heard that, he went away grieving, because he had many possessions.

POSSESSIONS AND THE KINGDOM

23 Jesus said to his disciples, "Truly I tell you, it will be hard for a rich person to enter the kingdom of heaven. 24 Again I tell you, it is easier for a camel to go through the eye of a needle than for a rich person to enter the kingdom of God."

25 When the disciples heard this, they were utterly astonished and asked, "Then who can be saved?"

26 Jesus looked at them and said, "With man this is impossible, but with God all things are possible."

27 Then Peter responded to him, "See, we have left everything and followed you. So what will there be for us?"

28 Jesus said to them, "Truly I tell you, in the renewal of all things, when the Son of Man sits on his glorious throne,

you who have followed me will also sit on twelve thrones, judging the twelve tribes of Israel. 29 And everyone who has left houses or brothers or sisters or father or mother or children or fields because of my name will receive a hundred times more and will inherit eternal life. 30 But many who are first will be last, and the last first."

Matthew 20

THE PARABLE OF THE VINEYARD WORKERS

1 "For the kingdom of heaven is like a landowner who went out early in the morning to hire workers for his vineyard. 2 After agreeing with the workers on one denarius, he sent them into his vineyard for the day. 3 When he went out about nine in the morning, he saw others standing in the marketplace doing nothing. 4 He said to them, 'You also go into my vineyard, and I'll give you whatever is right.' So off they went. 5 About noon and about three, he went out again and did the same thing. 6 Then about five he went and found others standing around and said to them, 'Why have you been standing here all day doing nothing?'

7 "'Because no one hired us,' they said to him.

"'You also go into my vineyard,' he told them. 8 When evening came, the owner of the vineyard told his foreman, 'Call the workers and give them their pay, starting with the last and ending with the first.'

9 "When those who were hired about five came, they each received one denarius. 10 So when the first ones came, they assumed they would get more, but they also received a denarius each. 11 When they received it, they began to complain to the landowner: 12 'These last men put in one hour, and you made them equal to us who bore the burden of the day's work and the burning heat.'

13 "He replied to one of them, 'Friend, I'm doing you no wrong. Didn't you agree with me on a denarius? 14 Take what's yours and go. I want to give this last man the same as I gave you. 15 Don't I have the right to do what I want with what is mine? Are you jealous because I'm generous?'

16 "So the last will be first, and the first last."

THE THIRD PREDICTION OF HIS DEATH

17 While going up to Jerusalem, Jesus took the twelve disciples aside privately and said to them on the way, 18 "See, we are going up to Jerusalem. The Son of Man will be handed over to the chief priests and scribes, and they will condemn him to death. 19 They will hand him over to the Gentiles to be mocked, flogged, and crucified, and on the third day he will be raised."

SUFFERING AND SERVICE

20 Then the mother of Zebedee's sons approached him with her sons. She knelt down to ask him for something. 21 "What do you want?" he asked her.

"Promise," she said to him, "that these two sons of mine may sit, one on your right and the other on your left, in your kingdom."

22 Jesus answered, "You don't know what you're asking. Are you able to drink the cup that I am about to drink?"

"We are able," they said to him.

23 He told them, "You will indeed drink my cup, but to sit at my right and left is not mine to give; instead, it is for those for whom it has been prepared by my Father."

24 When the ten disciples heard this, they became indignant with the two brothers. 25 Jesus called them over and said, "You know that the rulers of the Gentiles lord it over them, and those in high positions act as tyrants over them. 26 It must not be like that among you. On the contrary,

whoever wants to become great among you must be your servant,

27 and whoever wants to be first among you must be your slave; 28 just as the Son of Man did not come to be served, but to serve, and to give his life as a ransom for many."

TWO BLIND MEN HEALED

29 As they were leaving Jericho, a large crowd followed him. 30 There were two blind men sitting by the road. When they heard that Jesus was passing by, they cried out, "Lord, have

mercy on us, Son of David!" [31] The crowd demanded that they keep quiet, but they
cried out all the more, "Lord, have mercy on us, Son of David!"

NOTES

32 Jesus stopped, called them, and said, "What do you want me to do for you?"

33 "Lord," they said to him, "open our eyes." 34 Moved with compassion, Jesus
touched their eyes. Immediately they could see, and they followed him.

GOING DEEPER

Psalm 40:8

I delight to do your will, my God,
and your instruction is deep within me.

Philippians 2:5–11

CHRIST'S HUMILITY AND EXALTATION

5 Adopt the same attitude as that of Christ Jesus,

6 who, existing in the form of God,
did not consider equality with God
as something to be exploited.
7 Instead he emptied himself
by assuming the form of a servant,
taking on the likeness of humanity.
And when he had come as a man,
8 he humbled himself by becoming obedient
to the point of death—
even to death on a cross.
9 For this reason God highly exalted him
and gave him the name
that is above every name,
10 so that at the name of Jesus
every knee will bow—
in heaven and on earth
and under the earth—
11 and every tongue will confess
that Jesus Christ is Lord,
to the glory of God the Father.

DAY 19

JESUS *Is* KING

Matthew 21

THE TRIUMPHAL ENTRY

1 When they approached Jerusalem and came to
Bethphage at the Mount of Olives, Jesus then sent
two disciples, 2 telling them, "Go into the village
ahead of you. At once you will find a donkey tied
there with her colt. Untie them and bring them to
me. 3 If anyone says anything to you, say that the
Lord needs them, and he will send them at once."

4 This took place so that what was spoken through
the prophet might be fulfilled:

> 5 Tell Daughter Zion,
> "See, your King is coming to you,
> gentle, and mounted on a donkey,
> and on a colt,
> the foal of a donkey."

6 The disciples went and did just as Jesus directed
them. 7 They brought the donkey and the colt;
then they laid their clothes on them, and he sat
on them. 8 A very large crowd spread their clothes
on the road; others were cutting branches from
the trees and spreading them on the road. 9 Then
the crowds who went ahead of him and those who
followed shouted:

> *Hosanna* to the Son of David!
> Blessed is he who comes in the name
> of the Lord!
> *Hosanna* in the highest heaven!

10 When he entered Jerusalem, the whole city was
in an uproar, saying, "Who is this?" 11 The crowds
were saying, "This is the prophet Jesus from
Nazareth in Galilee."

CLEANSING THE TEMPLE

12 Jesus went into the temple and threw out all
those buying and selling. He overturned the tables
of the money changers and the chairs of those
selling doves. 13 He said to them, "It is written,
my house will be called a house of prayer, but you
are making it a den of thieves!"

CHILDREN PRAISE JESUS

14 The blind and the lame came to him in the
temple, and he healed them. 15 When the chief
priests and the scribes saw the wonders that he
did and the children shouting in the temple,
"*Hosanna* to the Son of David!" they were
indignant 16 and said to him, "Do you hear what
these children are saying?"

Jesus replied, "Yes, have you never read:

> You have prepared praise
> from the mouths of infants and
> nursing babies?"

17 Then he left them, went out of the city to
Bethany, and spent the night there.

THE BARREN FIG TREE

18 Early in the morning, as he was returning to
the city, he was hungry. 19 Seeing a lone fig tree by
the road, he went up to it and found nothing on
it except leaves. And he said to it, "May no fruit
ever come from you again!" At once the fig tree
withered.

20 When the disciples saw it, they were amazed
and said, "How did the fig tree wither so quickly?"

21 Jesus answered them, "Truly I tell you, if you
have faith and do not doubt, you will not only do
what was done to the fig tree, but even if you tell
this mountain, 'Be lifted up and thrown into the
sea,' it will be done. 22 And if you believe, you will
receive whatever you ask for in prayer."

What images are used to describe faith and a lack of faith?

21:18–22

THE AUTHORITY OF JESUS CHALLENGED

23 When he entered the temple, the chief priests
and the elders of the people came to him as he
was teaching and said, "By what authority are you
doing these things? Who gave you this authority?"

24 Jesus answered them, "I will also ask you
one question, and if you answer it for me,

then I will tell you by what authority I do these things. [25] Did John's baptism come from heaven, or was it of human origin?"

They discussed it among themselves, "If we say, 'From heaven,' he will say to us, 'Then why didn't you believe him?' [26] But if we say, 'Of human origin,' we're afraid of the crowd, because everyone considers John to be a prophet." [27] So they answered Jesus, "We don't know."

And he said to them, "Neither will I tell you by what authority I do these things.

THE PARABLE OF THE TWO SONS

[28] "What do you think? A man had two sons. He went to the first and said, 'My son, go work in the vineyard today.'

[29] "He answered, 'I don't want to,' but later he changed his mind and went. [30] Then the man went to the other and said the same thing. 'I will, sir,' he answered, but he didn't go. [31] Which of the two did his father's will?"

They said, "The first."

Jesus said to them, "Truly I tell you, tax collectors and prostitutes are entering the kingdom of God before you. [32] For John came to you in the way of righteousness, and you didn't believe him. Tax collectors and prostitutes did believe him; but you, when you saw it, didn't even change your minds then and believe him.

THE PARABLE OF THE VINEYARD OWNER

[33] "Listen to another parable: There was a landowner, who planted a vineyard, put a fence around it, dug a winepress in it, and built a watchtower. He leased it to tenant farmers and went away. [34] When the time came to harvest fruit, he sent his servants to the farmers to collect his fruit. [35] The farmers took his servants, beat one, killed another, and stoned a third. [36] Again, he sent other servants, more than the first group, and they did the same to them. [37] Finally, he sent his son to them. 'They will respect my son,' he said.

[38] "But when the tenant farmers saw the son, they said to each other, 'This is the heir. Come, let's kill him and take his inheritance.' [39] So they seized him, threw him out of the vineyard, and killed him. [40] Therefore, when the owner of the vineyard comes, what will he do to those farmers?"

[41] "He will completely destroy those terrible men," they told him, "and lease his vineyard to other farmers who will give him his fruit at the harvest."

[42] Jesus said to them, "Have you never read in the Scriptures:

> The stone that the builders rejected
> has become the cornerstone.
> This is what the Lord has done
> and it is wonderful in our eyes?

[43] Therefore I tell you, the kingdom of God will be taken away from you and given to a people producing its fruit. [44] Whoever falls on this stone will be broken to pieces; but on whomever it falls, it will shatter him."

[45] When the chief priests and the Pharisees heard his parables, they knew he was speaking about them. [46] Although they were looking for a way to arrest him, they feared the crowds, because the people regarded him as a prophet.

GOING DEEPER

Ezekiel 16:10–13

[10] "I clothed you in embroidered cloth and provided you with fine leather sandals. I also wrapped you in fine linen and covered you with silk. [11] I adorned you with jewelry, putting bracelets on your wrists and a necklace around your neck. [12] I put a ring in your nose, earrings on your ears, and a beautiful crown on your head. [13] So you were adorned with gold and silver, and your clothing was made of fine linen, silk, and embroidered cloth. You ate fine flour, honey, and oil. You became extremely beautiful and attained royalty."

Zechariah 9:9

Rejoice greatly, Daughter Zion!
Shout in triumph, Daughter Jerusalem!
Look, your King is coming to you;

he is righteous and victorious,
humble and riding on a donkey,
on a colt, the foal of a donkey.

NOTES

Colossians 1:15–20

THE CENTRALITY OF CHRIST

15 He is the image of the invisible God,
the firstborn over all creation.
16 For everything was created by him,
in heaven and on earth,
the visible and the invisible,
whether thrones or dominions
or rulers or authorities—
all things have been created through him and for him.
17 He is before all things,
and by him all things hold together.
18 He is also the head of the body, the church;
he is the beginning,
the firstborn from the dead,
so that he might come to have
first place in everything.
19 For God was pleased to have
all his fullness dwell in him,
20 and through him to reconcile
everything to himself,
whether things on earth or things in heaven,
by making peace
through his blood, shed on the cross.

GRACE *Day*

Take this day to catch up on your reading, pray, and rest in the presence of the Lord.

I delight to do your will,
my God, and your instruction
is deep within me.

Psalm 40:8

DAY
21

Weekly TRUTH

Scripture is God-breathed and true. When we memorize it, we carry the good news of Jesus with us wherever we go.

For this study we have worked to memorize our key verse in Matthew. Spend some time reading the full verse out loud and meditating on the good news of Jesus's message.

From then on Jesus began to preach, "Repent, because the kingdom of heaven has come near."

Matthew 4:17

See tips for memorizing Scripture on page 132.

DAY 22

Jesus NAMES *the* GREATEST *Commandments*

Matthew 22

THE PARABLE OF THE WEDDING BANQUET

1 Once more Jesus spoke to them in parables: 2 "The kingdom of heaven is like a king who gave a wedding banquet for his son. 3 He sent his servants to summon those invited to the banquet, but they didn't want to come. 4 Again, he sent out other servants and said, 'Tell those who are invited: See, I've prepared my dinner; my oxen and fattened cattle have been slaughtered, and everything is ready. Come to the wedding banquet.'

5 "But they paid no attention and went away, one to his own farm, another to his business, 6 while the rest seized his servants, mistreated them, and killed them. 7 The king was enraged, and he sent out his troops, killed those murderers, and burned down their city.

8 "Then he told his servants, 'The banquet is ready, but those who were invited were not worthy. 9 Go then to where the roads exit the city and invite everyone you find to the banquet.' 10 So those servants went out on the roads and gathered everyone they found, both evil and good. The wedding banquet was filled with guests. 11 When the king came in to see the guests, he saw a man there who was not dressed for a wedding. 12 So he said to him, 'Friend, how did you get in here without wedding clothes?' The man was speechless.

13 "Then the king told the attendants, 'Tie him up hand and foot, and throw him into the outer darkness, where there will be weeping and gnashing of teeth.'

14 "For many are invited, but few are chosen."

GOD AND CAESAR

15 Then the Pharisees went and plotted how to trap him by what he said. 16 So they sent their disciples to him, along with the Herodians. "Teacher," they said, "we know that you

NOTES

are truthful and teach truthfully the way of God. You don't care what anyone
thinks nor do you show partiality. [17] Tell us, then, what you think. Is it lawful to
pay taxes to Caesar or not?"

[18] Perceiving their malicious intent, Jesus said, "Why are you testing me, hypocrites?
[19] Show me the coin used for the tax." They brought him a denarius. [20] "Whose
image and inscription is this?" he asked them.

[21] "Caesar's," they said to him.

Then he said to them, "Give, then, to Caesar the things that are Caesar's, and to
God the things that are God's." [22] When they heard this, they were amazed. So they
left him and went away.

THE SADDUCEES AND THE RESURRECTION

[23] That same day some Sadducees, who say there is no resurrection, came up to him
and questioned him: [24] "Teacher, Moses said, if a man dies, having no children, his
brother is to marry his wife and raise up offspring for his brother. [25] Now there were
seven brothers among us. The first got married and died. Having no offspring, he
left his wife to his brother. [26] The same thing happened to the second also, and the
third, and so on to all seven. [27] Last of all, the woman died. [28] In the resurrection,
then, whose wife will she be of the seven? For they all had married her."

[29] Jesus answered them, "You are mistaken, because you don't know the Scriptures
or the power of God. [30] For in the resurrection they neither marry nor are given
in marriage but are like angels in heaven. [31] Now concerning the resurrection of
the dead, haven't you read what was spoken to you by God: [32] I am the God of
Abraham and the God of Isaac and the God of Jacob? He is not the God of the
dead, but of the living."

[33] And when the crowds heard this, they were astonished at his teaching.

THE PRIMARY COMMANDS

[34] When the Pharisees heard that he had silenced the Sadducees, they came
together. [35] And one of them, an expert in the law, asked a question to test him:
[36] "Teacher, which command in the law is the greatest?"

[37] He said to him,

"Love the Lord your God with all your heart,
with all your soul, and with all your mind.

[38] This is the greatest and most important command. [39] The second is like it:
Love your neighbor as yourself. [40] All the Law and the Prophets depend on these
two commands."

THE QUESTION ABOUT THE MESSIAH

[41] While the Pharisees were together, Jesus questioned them, [42] "What do you think about the Messiah? Whose son is he?"

They replied, "David's."

[43] He asked them, "How is it then that David, inspired by the Spirit, calls him 'Lord':

> [44] The Lord declared to my Lord,
> 'Sit at my right hand
> until I put your enemies under your feet'?

[45] "If David calls him 'Lord,' how, then, can he be his son?" [46] No one was able to answer him at all, and from that day no one dared to question him anymore.

GOING DEEPER

Deuteronomy 6:4–9

THE GREATEST COMMAND

[4] Listen, Israel: The LORD our God, the LORD is one. [5] Love the LORD your God
with all your heart, with all your soul, and with all your strength. [6] These words
that I am giving you today are to be in your heart. [7] Repeat them to your children.
Talk about them when you sit in your house and when you walk along the road,
when you lie down and when you get up. [8] Bind them as a sign on your hand and
let them be a symbol on your forehead. [9] Write them on the doorposts of your
house and on your city gates.

1 John 5:1–3

[1] Everyone who believes that Jesus is the Christ has been born of God, and everyone
who loves the Father also loves the one born of him. [2] This is how we know that
we love God's children: when we love God and obey his commands. [3] For this is
what love for God is: to keep his commands. And his commands are not a burden.

NOTES

DAY 23

JESUS *Rebukes the* RELIGIOUS LEADERS

"The greatest among you
will be your servant."

Matthew 23:11

Matthew 23

NOTES

RELIGIOUS HYPOCRITES DENOUNCED

1 Then Jesus spoke to the crowds and to his disciples: 2 "The scribes and the Pharisees are seated in the chair of Moses. 3 Therefore do whatever they tell you, and observe it.

But don't do what they do, because they don't practice what they teach.

4 They tie up heavy loads that are hard to carry and put them on people's shoulders, but they themselves aren't willing to lift a finger to move them. 5 They do everything to be seen by others: They enlarge their phylacteries and lengthen their tassels. 6 They love the place of honor at banquets, the front seats in the synagogues, 7 greetings in the marketplaces, and to be called 'Rabbi' by people.

8 "But you are not to be called 'Rabbi,' because you have one Teacher, and you are all brothers and sisters. 9 Do not call anyone on earth your father, because you have one Father, who is in heaven. 10 You are not to be called instructors either, because you have one Instructor, the Messiah. 11 The greatest among you will be your servant. 12 Whoever exalts himself will be humbled, and whoever humbles himself will be exalted.

13 "Woe to you, scribes and Pharisees, hypocrites! You shut the door of the kingdom of heaven in people's faces. For you don't go in, and you don't allow those entering to go in.

15 "Woe to you, scribes and Pharisees, hypocrites! You travel over land and sea to make one convert, and when he becomes one, you make him twice as much a child of hell as you are!

16 "Woe to you, blind guides, who say, 'Whoever takes an oath by the temple, it means nothing. But whoever takes an oath by the gold of the temple is bound by his oath.' 17 Blind fools! For which is greater, the gold or the temple that sanctified the gold? 18 Also, 'Whoever takes an oath by the altar, it means nothing; but whoever takes an oath by the gift that is on it is bound by his oath.' 19 Blind people! For which is greater, the gift or the altar that sanctifies the gift? 20 Therefore, the one who takes an oath by the altar takes an oath by it and by everything on it. 21 The one who takes an oath by the temple takes an oath by it and by him who dwells in it. 22 And the one who takes an oath by heaven takes an oath by God's throne and by him who sits on it.

23 "Woe to you, scribes and Pharisees, hypocrites! You pay a tenth of mint, dill, and cumin, and yet you have neglected the more important matters of the law—justice,

NOTES

mercy, and faithfulness. These things should have been done without neglecting the others. 24 Blind guides! You strain out a gnat, but gulp down a camel!

25 "Woe to you, scribes and Pharisees, hypocrites! You clean the outside of the cup and dish, but inside they are full of greed and self-indulgence. 26 Blind Pharisee! First clean the inside of the cup, so that the outside of it may also become clean.

27 "Woe to you, scribes and Pharisees, hypocrites! You are like whitewashed tombs, which appear beautiful on the outside, but inside are full of the bones of the dead and every kind of impurity. 28 In the same way, on the outside you seem righteous to people, but inside you are full of hypocrisy and lawlessness.

29 "Woe to you, scribes and Pharisees, hypocrites! You build the tombs of the prophets and decorate the graves of the righteous, 30 and you say, 'If we had lived in the days of our ancestors, we wouldn't have taken part with them in shedding the prophets' blood.' 31 So you testify against yourselves that you are descendants of those who murdered the prophets. 32 Fill up, then, the measure of your ancestors' sins!

33 "Snakes! Brood of vipers! How can you escape being condemned to hell? 34 This is why I am sending you prophets, sages, and scribes. Some of them you will kill and crucify, and some of them you will flog in your synagogues and pursue from town to town. 35 So all the righteous blood shed on the earth will be charged to you, from the blood of righteous Abel to the blood of Zechariah, son of Berechiah, whom you murdered between the sanctuary and the altar. 36 Truly I tell you, all these things will come on this generation.

JESUS'S LAMENTING OVER JERUSALEM

37 "Jerusalem, Jerusalem, who kills the prophets and stones those who are sent to her. How often I wanted to gather your children together, as a hen gathers her chicks under her wings, but you were not willing! 38 See, your house is left to you desolate. 39 For I tell you, you will not see me again until you say, 'Blessed is he who comes in the name of the Lord'!"

GOING DEEPER

Jeremiah 3:14–15

14 "Return, you faithless children—this is the LORD's declaration—for I am your master, and I will take you, one from a city and two from a family, and I will bring you to Zion. 15 I will give you shepherds who are loyal to me, and they will shepherd you with knowledge and skill."

NOTES

1 Peter 5:2–4

[2] Shepherd God's flock among you, not overseeing out of compulsion but willingly,
as God would have you; not out of greed for money but eagerly; [3] not lording it
over those entrusted to you, but being examples to the flock. [4] And when the chief
Shepherd appears, you will receive the unfading crown of glory.

DAY 24

JESUS *Teaches About His* RETURN

Matthew 24

DESTRUCTION OF THE TEMPLE PREDICTED

1 As Jesus left and was going out of the temple, his disciples came up and called his attention to its buildings. 2 He replied to them, "Do you see all these things? Truly I tell you, not one stone will be left here on another that will not be thrown down."

SIGNS OF THE END OF THE AGE

3 While he was sitting on the Mount of Olives, the disciples approached him privately and said, "Tell us, when will these things happen? And what is the sign of your coming and of the end of the age?"

4 Jesus replied to them, "Watch out that no one deceives you. 5 For many will come in my name, saying, 'I am the Messiah,' and they will deceive many. 6 You are going to hear of wars and rumors of wars. See that you are not alarmed, because these things must take place, but the end is not yet. 7 For nation will rise up against nation, and kingdom against kingdom. There will be famines and earthquakes in various places. 8 All these events are the beginning of labor pains.

PERSECUTIONS PREDICTED

9 "Then they will hand you over to be persecuted, and they will kill you. You will be hated by all nations because of my name. 10 Then many will fall away, betray one another, and hate one another. 11 Many false prophets will rise up and deceive many. 12 Because lawlessness will multiply, the love of many will grow cold. 13 But the one who endures to the end will be saved. 14 This good news of the kingdom will be proclaimed in all the world as a testimony to all nations, and then the end will come.

THE GREAT TRIBULATION

15 "So when you see the abomination of desolation, spoken of by the prophet Daniel, standing in the holy place" (let the reader understand), 16 "then those in Judea must flee to the mountains. 17 A man on the housetop must not come down to get things out of his house, 18 and a man in the field must not go back to get his coat. 19 Woe to pregnant women and nursing mothers in those days! 20 Pray that your escape may not be in winter or on a Sabbath. 21 For at that time there will be great distress, the kind that hasn't taken place from

NOTES

the beginning of the world until now and never will again. 22 Unless those days
were cut short, no one would be saved. But those days will be cut short because
of the elect.

23 "If anyone tells you then, 'See, here is the Messiah!' or, 'Over here!' do not
believe it. 24 For false messiahs and false prophets will arise and perform great signs
and wonders to lead astray, if possible, even the elect. 25 Take note: I have told you
in advance. 26 So if they tell you, 'See, he's in the wilderness!' don't go out; or, 'See,
he's in the storerooms!' do not believe it. 27 For as the lightning comes from the east
and flashes as far as the west, so will be the coming of the Son of Man. 28 Wherever
the carcass is, there the vultures will gather.

THE COMING OF THE SON OF MAN

29 "Immediately after the distress of those days, the sun will be darkened, and the
moon will not shed its light; the stars will fall from the sky, and the powers of the
heavens will be shaken. 30 Then the sign of the Son of Man will appear in the sky,
and then all the peoples of the earth will mourn; and they will see the Son of Man
coming on the clouds of heaven with power and great glory. 31 He will send out
his angels with a loud trumpet, and they will gather his elect from the four winds,
from one end of the sky to the other.

THE PARABLE OF THE FIG TREE

32 "Learn this lesson from the fig tree: As soon as its branch becomes tender and
sprouts leaves, you know that summer is near. 33 In the same way, when you see
all these things, recognize that he is near—at the door. 34 Truly I tell you, this
generation will certainly not pass away until all these things take place.

35 Heaven and earth will pass away, but my words will never pass away.

NO ONE KNOWS THE DAY OR HOUR

36 "Now concerning that day and hour no one knows—neither the angels of
heaven nor the Son —except the Father alone. 37 As the days of Noah were, so the
coming of the Son of Man will be. 38 For in those days before the flood they were
eating and drinking, marrying and giving in marriage, until the day Noah boarded
the ark. 39 They didn't know until the flood came and swept them all away. This is
the way the coming of the Son of Man will be. 40 Then two men will be in the field;
one will be taken and one left. 41 Two women will be grinding grain with a hand
mill; one will be taken and one left. 42 Therefore be alert, since you don't know
what day your Lord is coming. 43 But know this: If the homeowner had known
what time the thief was coming, he would have stayed alert and not let his house
be broken into. 44 This is why you are also to be ready, because the Son of Man is
coming at an hour you do not expect.

FAITHFUL SERVICE TO CHRIST

45 “Who then is a faithful and wise servant, whom his master has put in charge
of his household, to give them food at the proper time? 46 Blessed is that servant
whom the master finds doing his job when he comes. 47 Truly I tell you, he will put
him in charge of all his possessions. 48 But if that wicked servant says in his heart,
‘My master is delayed,’ 49 and starts to beat his fellow servants, and eats and drinks
with drunkards, 50 that servant’s master will come on a day he does not expect him
and at an hour he does not know. 51 He will cut him to pieces and assign him a
place with the hypocrites, where there will be weeping and gnashing of teeth.”

GOING DEEPER

Genesis 6:1–7

SONS OF GOD AND DAUGHTERS OF MANKIND

1 When mankind began to multiply on the earth and daughters were born to them,
2 the sons of God saw that the daughters of mankind were beautiful, and they took
any they chose as wives for themselves. 3 And the LORD said, “My Spirit will not
remain with mankind forever, because they are corrupt. Their days will be 120
years.” 4 The Nephilim were on the earth both in those days and afterward, when
the sons of God came to the daughters of mankind, who bore children to them.
They were the powerful men of old, the famous men.

JUDGMENT DECREED

5 When the LORD saw that human wickedness was widespread on the earth and
that every inclination of the human mind was nothing but evil all the time, 6 the
LORD regretted that he had made man on the earth, and he was deeply grieved.
7 Then the LORD said, “I will wipe mankind, whom I created, off the face of the
earth, together with the animals, creatures that crawl, and birds of the sky—for I
regret that I made them.”

Romans 13:12–14

12 The night is nearly over, and the day is near; so let us discard the deeds of darkness
and put on the armor of light. 13 Let us walk with decency, as in the daytime:
not in carousing and drunkenness; not in sexual impurity and promiscuity; not
in quarreling and jealousy. 14 But put on the Lord Jesus Christ, and make no
provision for the flesh to gratify its desires.

NOTES

Day

JESUS'S *Parable* ABOUT *the Kingdom of* GOD

25

Matthew 25

THE PARABLE OF THE TEN VIRGINS

1 "At that time the kingdom of heaven will be like ten virgins who took their lamps
and went out to meet the groom. 2 Five of them were foolish and five were wise.
3 When the foolish took their lamps, they didn't take oil with them; 4 but the wise
ones took oil in their flasks with their lamps. 5 When the groom was delayed, they
all became drowsy and fell asleep.

6 "In the middle of the night there was a shout: 'Here's the groom! Come out to
meet him.'

7 "Then all the virgins got up and trimmed their lamps. 8 The foolish ones said to
the wise ones, 'Give us some of your oil, because our lamps are going out.'

9 "The wise ones answered, 'No, there won't be enough for us and for you. Go
instead to those who sell oil, and buy some for yourselves.'

10 "When they had gone to buy some, the groom arrived, and those who were
ready went in with him to the wedding banquet, and the door was shut. 11 Later
the rest of the virgins also came and said, 'Master, master, open up for us!'

12 "He replied, 'Truly I tell you, I don't know you!'

13 "Therefore be alert, because you don't know either the day or the hour.

THE PARABLE OF THE TALENTS

14 "For it is just like a man about to go on a journey. He called his own servants
and entrusted his possessions to them. 15 To one he gave five talents, to another
two talents, and to another one talent, depending on each one's ability. Then he
went on a journey. Immediately 16 the man who had received five talents went, put
them to work, and earned five more. 17 In the same way the man with two earned
two more. 18 But the man who had received one talent went off, dug a hole in the
ground, and hid his master's money.

19 "After a long time the master of those servants came and settled accounts with
them. 20 The man who had received five talents approached, presented five more
talents, and said, 'Master, you gave me five talents. See, I've earned five more talents.'

21 "His master said to him, 'Well done, good and faithful servant! You were faithful
over a few things; I will put you in charge of many things. Share your master's joy.'

22 "The man with two talents also approached. He said, 'Master, you gave me two
talents. See, I've earned two more talents.'

What images are used to describe faith and a lack of faith?

25:1–13

NOTES

23 “His master said to him, ‘Well done, good and faithful servant! You were faithful
over a few things; I will put you in charge of many things. Share your master’s joy.’

24 “The man who had received one talent also approached and said, ‘Master, I know
you. You’re a harsh man, reaping where you haven’t sown and gathering where you
haven’t scattered seed. 25 So I was afraid and went off and hid your talent in the
ground. See, you have what is yours.’

26 “His master replied to him, ‘You evil, lazy servant! If you knew that I reap
where I haven’t sown and gather where I haven’t scattered, 27 then you should have
deposited my money with the bankers, and I would have received my money back
with interest when I returned.

28 “‘So take the talent from him and give it to the one who has ten talents. 29 For
to everyone who has, more will be given, and he will have more than enough. But
from the one who does not have, even what he has will be taken away from him.
30 And throw this good-for-nothing servant into the outer darkness, where there
will be weeping and gnashing of teeth.’

THE SHEEP AND THE GOATS

31 “When the Son of Man comes in his glory, and all the angels with him, then he
will sit on his glorious throne. 32 All the nations will be gathered before him, and
he will separate them one from another, just as a shepherd separates the sheep from
the goats. 33 He will put the sheep on his right and the goats on the left. 34 Then
the King will say to those on his right, ‘Come, you who are blessed by my Father;
inherit the kingdom prepared for you from the foundation of the world.

35 “‘For I was hungry and you gave me something to eat; I was thirsty and you
gave me something to drink; I was a stranger and you took me in; 36 I was naked
and you clothed me; I was sick and you took care of me; I was in prison and you
visited me.’

37 “Then the righteous will answer him, ‘Lord, when did we see you hungry and
feed you, or thirsty and give you something to drink? 38 When did we see you a
stranger and take you in, or without clothes and clothe you? 39 When did we see
you sick, or in prison, and visit you?’

40 “And the King will answer them, ‘Truly I tell you, whatever you did for one of
the least of these brothers and sisters of mine, you did for me.’

41 “Then he will also say to those on the left, ‘Depart from me, you who are cursed,

into the eternal fire prepared for the devil and his angels! 42 For I was hungry and
you gave me nothing to eat; I was thirsty and you gave me nothing to drink; 43 I
was a stranger and you didn't take me in; I was naked and you didn't clothe me,
sick and in prison and you didn't take care of me.'

NOTES

44 "Then they too will answer, 'Lord, when did we see you hungry, or thirsty, or a stranger, or without clothes, or sick, or in prison, and not help you?'

45 "Then he will answer them, 'Truly I tell you, whatever you did not do for one of the least of these, you did not do for me.'

46 "And they will go away into eternal punishment, but the righteous into eternal life."

GOING DEEPER

Isaiah 60:19–21

19 The sun will no longer be your light by day,
and the brightness of the moon will not shine on you.
The Lord will be your everlasting light,
and your God will be your splendor.
20 Your sun will no longer set,
and your moon will not fade;
for the Lord will be your everlasting light,
and the days of your sorrow will be over.
21 All your people will be righteous;
they will possess the land forever;
they are the branch I planted,
the work of my hands,
so that I may be glorified.

2 Peter 3:11–14

11 Since all these things are to be dissolved in this way, it is clear what sort of people
you should be in holy conduct and godliness 12 as you wait for the day of God and
hasten its coming. Because of that day, the heavens will be dissolved with fire and
the elements will melt with heat. 13 But based on his promise, we wait for new
heavens and a new earth, where righteousness dwells.

14 Therefore, dear friends, while you wait for these things, make every effort to be found without spot or blemish in his sight, at peace.

THE SABBATH *and Resurrection* SUNDAY

[We] have come to the possession of a new hope, no longer observing the Sabbath, but living in the observance of the Lord's day, on which also our life has sprung up again by him and by his death.

Ignatius of Antioch, AD 110

Again and again, the New Testament boldly proclaims that Jesus Christ's triumphant resurrection—displaying His power over death—was an event unlike any other the world has ever known. Resurrection Sunday changed every aspect of life for Jesus's followers, including the day of the week when they worshiped.

For centuries, the Jewish people gathered in worship to observe the Sabbath from sundown on Friday to sundown on Saturday. The marking of the Sabbath was instituted at creation and reinforced by the Ten Commandments. However, after Jesus conquered the grave by His resurrection, converts to Christianity began joining together to worship on Sundays.

This Matthew reading plan includes two additional days to finish reading about the resurrection on Sunday, to honor and mark the power of the resurrection. No matter where you are in the calendar year, we invite you to reflect and remember this holy weekend in real time as you read.

JESUS Is Arrested

DAY 26

Matthew 26

THE PLOT TO KILL JESUS

1 When Jesus had finished saying all these things, he told his disciples,
2 "You know that the Passover takes place after two days, and the Son of
Man will be handed over to be crucified."

3 Then the chief priests and the elders of the people assembled in the
courtyard of the high priest, who was named Caiaphas, 4 and they
conspired to arrest Jesus in a treacherous way and kill him. 5 "Not during
the festival," they said, "so there won't be rioting among the people."

THE ANOINTING AT BETHANY

6 While Jesus was in Bethany at the house of Simon the leper, 7 a
woman approached him with an alabaster jar of very expensive perfume.
She poured it on his head as he was reclining at the table. 8 When the
disciples saw it, they were indignant. "Why this waste?" they asked.
9 "This might have been sold for a great deal and given to the poor."

10 Aware of this, Jesus said to them, "Why are you bothering this woman?
She has done a noble thing for me. 11 You always have the poor with you,
but you do not always have me. 12 By pouring this perfume on my body,
she has prepared me for burial. 13 Truly I tell you, wherever this gospel
is proclaimed in the whole world, what she has done will also be told in
memory of her."

14 Then one of the Twelve, the man called Judas Iscariot, went to the chief
priests 15 and said, "What are you willing to give me if I hand him over to
you?" So they weighed out thirty pieces of silver for him. 16 And from that
time he started looking for a good opportunity to betray him.

BETRAYAL AT THE PASSOVER

17 On the first day of Unleavened Bread the disciples came to Jesus and asked,
"Where do you want us to make preparations for you to eat the Passover?"

18 "Go into the city to a certain man," he said, "and tell him, 'The Teacher
says: My time is near; I am celebrating the Passover at your place with my
disciples.'" 19 So the disciples did as Jesus had directed them and prepared
the Passover. 20 When evening came, he was reclining at the table with the
Twelve. 21 While they were eating, he said, "Truly I tell you, one of you
will betray me."

22 Deeply distressed, each one began to say to him, "Surely not I, Lord?"

NOTES

23 He replied, "The one who dipped his hand with me in the bowl—he will betray
me. 24 The Son of Man will go just as it is written about him, but woe to that man
by whom the Son of Man is betrayed! It would have been better for him if he had
not been born."

25 Judas, his betrayer, replied, "Surely not I, Rabbi?"

"You have said it," he told him.

THE FIRST LORD'S SUPPER

26 As they were eating, Jesus took bread, blessed and broke it, gave it to the
disciples, and said, "Take and eat it; this is my body." 27 Then he took a cup, and
after giving thanks, he gave it to them and said, "Drink from it, all of you. 28 For
this is my blood of the covenant, which is poured out for many for the forgiveness
of sins. 29 But I tell you, I will not drink from this fruit of the vine from now on
until that day when I drink it new with you in my Father's kingdom." 30 After
singing a hymn, they went out to the Mount of Olives.

PETER'S DENIAL PREDICTED

31 Then Jesus said to them, "Tonight all of you will fall away because of me, for it
is written:

> I will strike the shepherd,
> and the sheep of the flock will be scattered.

32 But after I have risen, I will go ahead of you to Galilee."

33 Peter told him, "Even if everyone falls away because of you, I will never fall away."

34 "Truly I tell you," Jesus said to him, "tonight, before the rooster crows, you will
deny me three times."

35 "Even if I have to die with you," Peter told him, "I will never deny you," and all
the disciples said the same thing.

THE PRAYER IN THE GARDEN

36 Then Jesus came with them to a place called Gethsemane, and he told the
disciples, "Sit here while I go over there and pray." 37 Taking along Peter and the
two sons of Zebedee, he began to be sorrowful and troubled. 38 He said to them,
"I am deeply grieved to the point of death. Remain here and stay awake with me."
39 Going a little farther, he fell facedown and prayed, "My Father, if it is possible,
let this cup pass from me. Yet not as I will, but as you will."

40 Then he came to the disciples and found them sleeping. He asked Peter, "So, couldn't you stay awake with me one hour? 41 Stay awake and pray, so that you won't enter into temptation. The spirit is willing, but the flesh is weak."

42 Again, a second time, he went away and prayed, "My Father, if this cannot pass unless I drink it, your will be done." 43 And he came again and found them sleeping, because they could not keep their eyes open.

44 After leaving them, he went away again and prayed a third time, saying the same thing once more. 45 Then he came to the disciples and said to them, "Are you still sleeping and resting? See, the time is near. The Son of Man is betrayed into the hands of sinners. 46 Get up; let's go. See, my betrayer is near."

JUDAS'S BETRAYAL OF JESUS

47 While he was still speaking, Judas, one of the Twelve, suddenly arrived. A large mob with swords and clubs was with him from the chief priests and elders of the people. 48 His betrayer had given them a sign: "The one I kiss, he's the one; arrest him." 49 So immediately he went up to Jesus and said, "Greetings, Rabbi!" and kissed him.

50 "Friend," Jesus asked him, "why have you come?"

Then they came up, took hold of Jesus, and arrested him. 51 At that moment one of those with Jesus reached out his hand and drew his sword. He struck the high priest's servant and cut off his ear.

52 Then Jesus told him, "Put your sword back in its place because all who take up the sword will perish by the sword. 53 Or do you think that I cannot call on my Father, and he will provide me here and now with more than twelve legions of angels? 54 How, then, would the Scriptures be fulfilled that say it must happen this way?"

55 At that time Jesus said to the crowds, "Have you come out with swords and clubs, as if I were a criminal, to capture me? Every day I used to sit, teaching in the temple, and you didn't arrest me. 56 But all this has happened so that the writings of the prophets would be fulfilled." Then all the disciples deserted him and ran away.

JESUS FACES THE SANHEDRIN

57 Those who had arrested Jesus led him away to Caiaphas the high priest, where the scribes and the elders had convened. 58 Peter was following him at a distance right to the high priest's courtyard. He went in and was sitting with the servants to see the outcome.

59 The chief priests and the whole Sanhedrin were looking for false testimony against Jesus so that they could put him to death, 60 but they could not find any, even though many false witnesses came forward. Finally, two who came forward 61 stated, "This man said, 'I can destroy the temple of God and rebuild it in three days.'"

62 The high priest stood up and said to him, "Don't you have an answer to what these men are testifying against you?" 63 But Jesus kept silent. The high priest said to him, "I charge you under oath by the living God: Tell us if you are the Messiah, the Son of God."

64 "You have said it," Jesus told him.

"But I tell you, in the future you will see the Son of Man seated at the right hand of Power and coming on the clouds of heaven."

65 Then the high priest tore his robes and said, "He has blasphemed! Why do we still need witnesses? See, now you've heard the blasphemy. 66 What is your decision?"

They answered, "He deserves death!" 67 Then they spat in his face and beat him; others slapped him 68 and said, "Prophesy to us, Messiah! Who was it that hit you?"

PETER DENIES HIS LORD

69 Now Peter was sitting outside in the courtyard. A servant girl approached him and said, "You were with Jesus the Galilean too."

70 But he denied it in front of everyone: "I don't know what you're talking about."

NOTES

71 When he had gone out to the gateway, another woman saw him and told those
who were there, "This man was with Jesus the Nazarene!"

72 And again he denied it with an oath: "I don't know the man!"

73 After a little while those standing there approached and said to Peter, "You really
are one of them, since even your accent gives you away."

74 Then he started to curse and to swear with an oath, "I don't know the man!"
Immediately a rooster crowed, 75 and Peter remembered the words Jesus had
spoken, "Before the rooster crows, you will deny me three times." And he went
outside and wept bitterly.

GOING DEEPER

Daniel 7:13–14

13 I continued watching in the night visions,

and suddenly one like a son of man
was coming with the clouds of heaven.
He approached the Ancient of Days
and was escorted before him.
14 He was given dominion
and glory and a kingdom,
so that those of every people,
nation, and language
should serve him.
His dominion is an everlasting dominion
that will not pass away,
and his kingdom is one
that will not be destroyed.

1 Corinthians 2:7–8

7 On the contrary, we speak God's hidden wisdom in a mystery, a wisdom God
predestined before the ages for our glory. 8 None of the rulers of this age knew
this wisdom, because if they had known it, they would not have crucified the
Lord of glory.

Jesus Is CRUCIFIED

DAY 27

Matthew 27

JESUS HANDED OVER TO PILATE

1 When daybreak came, all the chief priests and the elders of the people plotted against Jesus to put him to death. 2 After tying him up, they led him away and handed him over to Pilate, the governor.

JUDAS HANGS HIMSELF

3 Then Judas, his betrayer, seeing that Jesus had been condemned, was full of remorse and returned the thirty pieces of silver to the chief priests and elders. 4 "I have sinned by betraying innocent blood," he said.

"What's that to us?" they said. "See to it yourself!" 5 So he threw the silver into the temple and departed. Then he went and hanged himself.

6 The chief priests took the silver and said, "It's not permitted to put it into the temple treasury, since it is blood money." 7 They conferred together and bought the potter's field with it as a burial place for foreigners. 8 Therefore that field has been called "Field of Blood" to this day. 9 Then what was spoken through the prophet Jeremiah was fulfilled: They took the thirty pieces of silver, the price of him whose price was set by the Israelites, 10 and they gave them for the potter's field, as the Lord directed me.

JESUS FACES THE GOVERNOR

11 Now Jesus stood before the governor. "Are you the king of the Jews?" the governor asked him.

Jesus answered, "You say so." 12 While he was being accused by the chief priests and elders, he didn't answer.

13 Then Pilate said to him, "Don't you hear how much they are testifying against you?" 14 But he didn't answer him on even one charge, so that the governor was quite amazed.

JESUS OR BARABBAS

15 At the festival the governor's custom was to release to the crowd a prisoner they wanted. 16 At that time they had a notorious prisoner called Barabbas. 17 So when they had gathered together, Pilate said to them, "Who is it you want me to release for you—Barabbas, or Jesus who is called Christ?" 18 For he knew it was because of envy that they had handed him over.

19 While he was sitting on the judge's bench, his wife sent word to him, "Have nothing to do with that righteous man, for today I've suffered terribly in a dream because of him."

20 The chief priests and the elders, however, persuaded the crowds to ask for Barabbas and to execute Jesus. 21 The governor asked them, "Which of the two do you want me to release for you?"

"Barabbas!" they answered.

22 Pilate asked them, "What should I do then with Jesus, who is called Christ?"

They all answered, "Crucify him!"

23 Then he said, "Why? What has he done wrong?"

But they kept shouting all the more, "Crucify him!"

24 When Pilate saw that he was getting nowhere, but that a riot was starting instead, he took some water, washed his hands in front of the crowd, and said, "I am innocent of this man's blood. See to it yourselves!"

25 All the people answered, "His blood be on us and on our children!" 26 Then he released Barabbas to them and, after having Jesus flogged, handed him over to be crucified.

MOCKED BY THE MILITARY

27 Then the governor's soldiers took Jesus into the governor's residence and gathered the whole company around him. 28 They stripped him and dressed him in a scarlet robe. 29 They twisted together a crown of thorns, put it on his head, and placed a staff in his right hand. And they knelt down before him and mocked him: "Hail, king of the Jews!" 30 Then they spat on him, took the staff, and kept hitting him on the head. 31 After they had mocked him, they stripped him of the robe, put his own clothes on him, and led him away to crucify him.

CRUCIFIED BETWEEN TWO CRIMINALS

32 As they were going out, they found a Cyrenian man named Simon. They forced him to carry his cross. 33 When they came to a place called *Golgotha* (which means Place of the Skull), 34 they gave him wine mixed with gall to drink. But when he tasted it, he refused to drink it. 35 After crucifying him, they divided his clothes by casting lots. 36 Then they sat down and were guarding him there. 37 Above his head they put up the charge against him in writing: THIS IS JESUS, THE KING OF THE JEWS.

38 Then two criminals were crucified with him, one on the right and one on the left. 39 Those who passed by were yelling insults at him, shaking their heads 40 and saying, "You who would destroy the temple and rebuild it in three days, save yourself! If you are the Son of God, come down from the cross!" 41 In the same way the chief priests, with the scribes and elders, mocked him and said, 42 "He saved others, but he cannot save himself! He is the King of Israel! Let him come down now from the cross, and we will believe in him. 43 He trusts in God; let God rescue him now—if he takes pleasure in him! For he said, 'I am the Son of God.'" 44 In the same way even the criminals who were crucified with him taunted him.

THE DEATH OF JESUS

45 From noon until three in the afternoon, darkness came over the whole land. 46 About three in the afternoon Jesus cried out with a loud voice, *"Elí, Elí, lemá sabachtháni?"* that is, "My God, my God, why have you abandoned me?"

47 When some of those standing there heard this, they said, "He's calling for Elijah."

48 Immediately one of them ran and got a sponge, filled it with sour wine, put it on a stick, and offered him a drink. 49 But the rest said, "Let's see if Elijah comes to save him."

50 But Jesus cried out again with a loud voice and gave up his spirit. 51 Suddenly, the curtain of the sanctuary was torn in two from top to bottom, the earth quaked, and the rocks were split. 52 The tombs were also opened and many bodies of the saints who had fallen asleep were raised. 53 And they came out of the tombs after his resurrection, entered the holy city, and appeared to many.

54 When the centurion and those with him, who were keeping watch over Jesus, saw the earthquake and the things that had happened, they were terrified and said, "Truly this man was the Son of God!"

55 Many women who had followed Jesus from Galilee and looked after him were there, watching from a distance. 56 Among them were Mary Magdalene, Mary the mother of James and Joseph, and the mother of Zebedee's sons.

THE BURIAL OF JESUS

57 When it was evening, a rich man from Arimathea named Joseph came, who himself had also become a disciple of Jesus. 58 He approached Pilate and asked for Jesus's body. Then Pilate ordered that it be released. 59 So Joseph took the body, wrapped it in clean, fine linen, 60 and placed it in his new tomb, which he had cut into the rock. He left after rolling a great stone against the entrance of the tomb. 61 Mary Magdalene and the other Mary were seated there, facing the tomb.

THE CLOSELY GUARDED TOMB

62 The next day, which followed the preparation day, the chief priests and the Pharisees gathered before Pilate 63 and said, "Sir, we remember that while this deceiver was still alive he said, 'After three days I will rise again.' 64 So give orders that the tomb be made secure until the third day. Otherwise, his disciples may come, steal him, and tell the people, 'He has been raised from the dead,' and the last deception will be worse than the first."

65 "Take guards," Pilate told them. "Go and make it as secure as you know how." 66 They went and secured the tomb by setting a seal on the stone and placing the guards.

GOING DEEPER

Isaiah 53:1–9

1 Who has believed what we have heard?
And to whom has the arm of the LORD been revealed?
2 He grew up before him like a young plant
and like a root out of dry ground.

He didn't have an impressive form
or majesty that we should look at him,
no appearance that we should desire him.
3 He was despised and rejected by men,
a man of suffering who knew what sickness was.
He was like someone people turned away from;
he was despised, and we didn't value him.

4 Yet he himself bore our sicknesses,
and he carried our pains;
but we in turn regarded him stricken,
struck down by God, and afflicted.
5 But he was pierced because of our rebellion,
crushed because of our iniquities;
punishment for our peace was on him,
and we are healed by his wounds.
6 We all went astray like sheep;
we all have turned to our own way;
and the LORD has punished him
for the iniquity of us all.

7 He was oppressed and afflicted,
yet he did not open his mouth.
Like a lamb led to the slaughter
and like a sheep silent before her shearers,
he did not open his mouth.
8 He was taken away because of oppression and judgment,
and who considered his fate?
For he was cut off from the land of the living;
he was struck because of my people's rebellion.
9 He was assigned a grave with the wicked,
but he was with a rich man at his death,
because he had done no violence
and had not spoken deceitfully.

John 3:16

"For God loved the world in this way: He gave his one and only Son, so that everyone who believes in him will not perish but have eternal life."

Day 28

Jesus Is RESURRECTED

He is not here. For he has risen,
just as he said.

Matthew 28:5

NOTES

Matthew 28

RESURRECTION MORNING

1 After the Sabbath, as the first day of the week was dawning, Mary Magdalene and
the other Mary went to view the tomb. 2 There was a violent earthquake, because
an angel of the Lord descended from heaven and approached the tomb. He rolled
back the stone and was sitting on it. 3 His appearance was like lightning, and his
clothing was as white as snow. 4 The guards were so shaken by fear of him that they
became like dead men.

5 The angel told the women,

"Don't be afraid, because I know you are looking
for Jesus who was crucified.

6 He is not here. For he has risen, just as he said. Come and see the place where
he lay. 7 Then go quickly and tell his disciples, 'He has risen from the dead and
indeed he is going ahead of you to Galilee; you will see him there.' Listen, I have
told you."

8 So, departing quickly from the tomb with fear and great joy, they ran to tell his
disciples the news. 9 Just then Jesus met them and said, "Greetings!" They came
up, took hold of his feet, and worshiped him. 10 Then Jesus told them, "Do not be
afraid. Go and tell my brothers to leave for Galilee, and they will see me there."

THE SOLDIERS BRIBED TO LIE

11 As they were on their way, some of the guards came into the city and reported to
the chief priests everything that had happened. 12 After the priests had assembled
with the elders and agreed on a plan, they gave the soldiers a large sum of money
13 and told them, "Say this, 'His disciples came during the night and stole him
while we were sleeping.' 14 If this reaches the governor's ears, we will deal with
him and keep you out of trouble." 15 They took the money and did as they were
instructed, and this story has been spread among Jewish people to this day.

THE GREAT COMMISSION

16 The eleven disciples traveled to Galilee, to the mountain where Jesus had
directed them. 17 When they saw him, they worshiped, but some doubted. 18 Jesus
came near and said to them, "All authority has been given to me in heaven and
on earth. 19 Go, therefore, and make disciples of all nations, baptizing them in
the name of the Father and of the Son and of the Holy Spirit, 20 teaching them to
observe everything I have commanded you. And remember, I am with you always,
to the end of the age."

NOTES

Psalm 16:8–11

[8] I always let the Lord guide me.
Because he is at my right hand,
I will not be shaken.

[9] Therefore my heart is glad
and my whole being rejoices;
my body also rests securely.
[10] For you will not abandon me to Sheol;
you will not allow your faithful one to see decay.
[11] You reveal the path of life to me;
in your presence is abundant joy;
at your right hand are eternal pleasures.

1 Corinthians 15:1–4

RESURRECTION ESSENTIAL TO THE GOSPEL

[1] Now I want to make clear for you, brothers and sisters, the gospel I preached to
you, which you received, on which you have taken your stand [2] and by which you
are being saved, if you hold to the message I preached to you—unless you believed
in vain. [3] For I passed on to you as most important what I also received: that Christ
died for our sins according to the Scriptures, [4] that he was buried, that he was
raised on the third day according to the Scriptures.

RESPOND

We've arrived at Resurrection Sunday and now celebrate the new life we have because of our risen Savior. Along the way, we've looked at what it means to have true faith in Christ, and what that means for how we live our lives.

Look back over your notes from the last four weeks. What patterns or consistent actions, images, or themes did you observe about how Jesus depicts faith in action in His teaching and ministry?

01

What temptations, doubts, or distractions do you see in your own life that are obstacles to faith?

02

Moving forward, what can you do to remember the kind of faith Jesus describes? How do you want to live differently because of the perspectives and images Jesus gave to describe an active faith?

03

Benediction

She will give BIRTH *to a* SON, *and* YOU *are to* NAME *him* JESUS, BECAUSE *he* WILL SAVE *his* PEOPLE *from their sins.*

MATTHEW 1:21

Tips for Memorizing Scripture

At She Reads Truth, we believe Scripture memorization is an important discipline in your walk with God. Committing God's Truth to memory means He can minister to us—and we can minister to others—through His Word no matter where we are. As you approach the Weekly Truth passage in this book, try these memorization tips to see which techniques work best for you!

STUDY IT

Study the passage in its biblical context and ask yourself a few questions before you begin to memorize it: What does this passage say? What does it mean? How would I say this in my own words? What does it teach me about God? Understanding what the passage means helps you know why it is important to carry it with you wherever you go.

Break the passage into smaller sections, memorizing a phrase at a time.

PRAY IT

Use the passage you are memorizing as a prompt for prayer.

WRITE IT

Dedicate a notebook to Scripture memorization and write the passage over and over again.

Diagram the passage after you write it out. Place a square around the verbs, underline the nouns, and circle any adjectives or adverbs. Say the passage aloud several times, emphasizing the verbs as you repeat it. Then do the same thing again with the nouns, then the adjectives and adverbs.

Write out the first letter of each word in the passage somewhere you can reference it throughout the week as you work on your memorization.

Use a whiteboard to write out the passage. Erase a few words at a time as you continue to repeat it aloud. Keep erasing parts of the passage until you have it all committed to memory.

CREATE

If you can, make up a tune for the passage to sing as you go about your day, or try singing it to the tune of a favorite song.

Sketch the passage, visualizing what each phrase would look like in the form of a picture. Or, try using calligraphy or altering the style of your handwriting as you write it out.

Use hand signals or signs to come up with associations for each word or phrase and repeat the movements as you practice.

SAY IT

Repeat the passage out loud to yourself as you are going through the rhythm of your day—getting ready, pouring your coffee, waiting in traffic, or making dinner.

Listen to the passage read aloud to you.

Record a voice memo on your phone and listen to it throughout the day or play it on an audio Bible.

SHARE IT

Memorize the passage with a friend, family member, or mentor. Spontaneously challenge each other to recite the passage, or pick a time to review your passage and practice saying it from memory together.

Send the passage as an encouraging text to a friend, testing yourself as you type to see how much you have memorized so far.

KEEP AT IT!

Set reminders on your phone to prompt you to practice your passage.

Purchase a She Reads Truth 12 Card Set or keep a stack of note cards with Scripture you are memorizing by your bed. Practice reciting what you've memorized previously before you go to sleep, ending with the passages you are currently learning. If you wake up in the middle of the night, review them again instead of grabbing your phone. Read them out loud before you get out of bed in the morning.

CSB BOOK ABBREVIATIONS

OLD TESTAMENT

GN Genesis
EX Exodus
LV Leviticus
NM Numbers
DT Deuteronomy
JOS Joshua
JDG Judges
RU Ruth
1SM 1 Samuel
2SM 2 Samuel
1KG 1 Kings
2KG 2 Kings
1CH 1 Chronicles
2CH 2 Chronicles
EZR Ezra
NEH Nehemiah
EST Esther
JB Job
PS Psalms
PR Proverbs
EC Ecclesiastes
SG Song of Solomon
IS Isaiah
JR Jeremiah
LM Lamentations
EZK Ezekiel
DN Daniel
HS Hosea
JL Joel
AM Amos
OB Obadiah
JNH Jonah
MC Micah
NAH Nahum
HAB Habakkuk
ZPH Zephaniah
HG Haggai
ZCH Zechariah
MAL Malachi

NEW TESTAMENT

MT Matthew
MK Mark
LK Luke
JN John
AC Acts
RM Romans
1CO 1 Corinthians
2CO 2 Corinthians
GL Galatians
EPH Ephesians
PHP Philippians
COL Colossians
1TH 1 Thessalonians
2TH 2 Thessalonians
1TM 1 Timothy
2TM 2 Timothy
TI Titus
PHM Philemon
HEB Hebrews
JMS James
1PT 1 Peter
2PT 2 Peter
1JN 1 John
2JN 2 John
3JN 3 John
JD Jude
RV Revelation

BIBLIOGRAPHY

Cox, Homersham. *The First Century of Christianity*, 322. London: Longmans, Green & Company, 1886.

France, R. T. *Matthew: An Introduction and Commentary*. Vol. 1. Tyndale New Testament Commentaries. Downers Grove: InterVarsity Press, 1985.

Kugler, Chris. "Faith," in *Lexham Theological Wordbook*, ed. Douglas Mangum et al., Lexham Bible Reference Series. Bellingham: Lexham Press, 2014.

Manser, Martin H. *Dictionary of Bible Themes: The Accessible and Comprehensive Tool for Topical Studies*. London: Martin Manser, 2009.

Platt, David. *Christ-Centered Exposition Commentary: Exalting Jesus in Matthew*, ed. Daniel L. Akin, David Platt, and Tony Merida, 69–70. Nashville: Holman Reference, 2013.

You just spent 28 days in the Word of God!

MY FAVORITE DAY OF THIS READING PLAN:

ONE THING I LEARNED ABOUT GOD:

WHAT WAS GOD DOING IN MY LIFE DURING THIS STUDY?

HOW DID I FIND DELIGHT IN GOD'S WORD?

WHAT DID I LEARN THAT I WANT TO SHARE WITH SOMEONE ELSE?

A SPECIFIC PASSAGE OR VERSE THAT ENCOURAGED ME:

A SPECIFIC PASSAGE OR VERSE THAT CHALLENGED AND CONVICTED ME: